Tamara Łozińs

WARSAW

149 colour illustrations

BONECHI

Dystrybutor w Polsce:
"GALAKTYKA" SP. Z O. O. Łódź
Fax. 42 791335 - Tel. 42 406509

ISBN 83-86447-15-X

Printed in Italy
by Centro Stampa Editoriale Bonechi.

Translated by Marzenna Rączkowska

CREDITS
Photographs from the Archives
of Casa Editrice Bonechi
were taken by Andrea Pistolesi.

ISBN 88-8029-317-6

* * *

Old Town walls

INTRODUCTION

The first settlements in what is now Warsaw were formed in the 10th and 11th centuries. Toward the end of the 13th century a stronghold was established, serving as the seat of the Mazowsze Dukes. Soon a town was set up, which together with the stronghold bore the name of Warszowa (this was the original and until the 17th century the only name of present-day Warszawa). In the 1430's the town was already built up and fortified. A century later, the role of Warsaw as a political centre increased — its rank was raised to that of the capital of the Mazowsze region. In 1526, after the extinction of the Mazowsze Dukes' dynasty, the region they had ruled became incorporated into the Crown.

The political significance of the city increased steadily throughout the 16th century, largely due to its central position in the country: after 1569 Warsaw became the venue for the General Seym (Parliamentary) Meetings of the Republic, and since 1573 elections of Polish Kings were also held there. Finally, in 1573 King Sigismundus Vasa III made the decision to permanently transfer the royal residence and the main state offices from Cracow to Warsaw.

The process of transforming the city into the capital of Poland resulted in its considerable development and expansion. Many beautiful magnate residences were built in the suburbs. Under the rule of the Vasas, Warsaw was not only the political and administrative capital of the country, but — thanks to royal and magnate patronage — it also became the main centre of science, art and culture.

Wars with Sweden in the mid 17th century caused a slump in the growth of the city; between 1655—1658 Warsaw incurred heavy losses due to several sieges, defeats, and Swedish occupation. Fortunately, after liberation it was quite quickly rebuilt. One of the people taking part in its restoration was the outstanding architect of Dutch origin, Tylman of Gameren, who was brought to Poland by Marshall Stanisław Herakliusz Lubomirski. His works included palaces of the Krasiński and Gniński (Ostrogski) families and the commercial centre erected on the initiative of Queen Maria Kazimiera, called Marywil (pulled down in 1825). King Jan Sobieski III's suburban residence of Wilanów was also built in the second part of the 17th century. The wars of the early 18th century as well as pestilence brought about a second slump in the development of the city.

A period of peace started in 1716, enabling Warsaw to flourish once again. Great urban projects were made under the rule of Kings from the Saxon Dynasty — Augustus II and Augustus III: the Saxon Axis (the Saxon Garden is what remains of them to this day) and the Calvary Road (the present Al. Ujazdowskie) which was the natural extension of the route leading from the Old Town to the Royal Castle by way of Krakowskie Przedmieście and Nowy Świat to Wilanów. New palaces and churches were erected. Since 1742 city cleanliness became the responsibility of the Cobblestone Committee run by Marshall Franciszek Bieliński.

In the times of Stanislaus Augustus, Warsaw was the centre of the Enlightenment in Poland. All the brightest minds of the period, who aimed carrying out reforms and strengthening the country internally were concentrated around the King. Building the palace complex in the Łazienki Park and restructuring the Royal Castle interiors was carried out on the King's initiative.

Cultural and scientific activities which were to maintain the feeling of national identity in a society deprived of its state were continued throughout the period of the partitions. Some of the centres of such activities were the Polish theatre and the Friends of Science Society. Despite the partitions, the latter represented the science of the whole country. Besides, Warsaw became the centre of independence movements undertaken by many underground organizations, mainly assembling young people. These activities led to the outbreak of the November Uprising of 1830. Its defeat brought the development of the city to an end. A period of political terror began. Institutions of higher education and science institutes were closed, art collections sent out of the city, cultural activities prohibited. After 1860 Warsaw again became a place of patriotic manifestations leading to the outbreak of the January Uprising of 1863. During the uprising it was the seat of the National Rebel Government. When it fell, the Polish autonomous government was overthrown and the city's government was taken over by Russian administration.

It was only after the end of World War I in 1918, that Warsaw regained the rank of an independent state's capital. The Second World War and German occupation brought about losses far greater than ever before. A total annihilation of the city took place after the Warsaw Uprising of 1944, when Germans blew up all the remaining buildings, changing the capital of Poland into an expanse of ruins and rubble.

Reconstruction was started immediately after liberation. All the historical complexes and buildings were meticulously restored, and great effort was made to restore their original form and appearance. The Old and New Town, Krakowskie Przedmieście, Nowy Świat, Aleje Ujazdowskie, the regions of Długa, Miodowa and Senatorska Streets were all rebuilt. The panorama of the Old Town seen from the Vistula River, the palaces and churches situated along the embankment, as well as Aleje Ujazdowskie flanked with elegant houses and greenery, once again became the most beautiful parts of the city.

The Castle, western wall

ROYAL CASTLE

The history of the Warsaw Castle dates back to the 13th century. A masonry Great Tower (later called the Grodzka, i.e. Civic Tower) was erected in the first half of the 14th century; in the years 1411–1413, under the reign of Duke Janusz I the Eleder, a masonry ducal residence later called The Major Court (Curia Maior) was added. It had an adjoining round tower containing a staircase. More masonry buildings were erected over the 15th century: defense walls, and the so-called Smaller Court (Curia Minor).

After the extinction of the Mazowsze Dukes, their Duchy was incorporated into the Crown and the castle became a royal residence.

The reign of Sigismundus Augustus initiated the process of transferring the main centre of power in the Republic from Cracow to Warsaw, and in 1569 the decision was made to transfer meetings of the Seym there. The new functions of the town required considerable extension of the royal residence. In the years 1569–1572, the Major Court was rebuilt and adjusted to the needs of housing the Seym of the Republic. It was extended by a one storey building erected at an obtuse angle to the Major Court and containing royal chambers which could be reached by means of a staircase situated in a separate tower. Also the

Smaller Court, occupied by Sigismundus Augustus' sister Anna, was redesigned and modernised. Work was interrupted by the King's death in 1572.

The next phase of enlarging the castle fell on the reign of the Vasas; it was initiated by King Sigismundus III. Started in 1598, the work lasted until 1619, but in the main part the residence was probably finished by 1611, the year the King and his main offices moved to Warsaw from Cracow. After the extension, the castle was pentagonal in shape, with an internal courtyard, which in its main outline was preserved until 1939. The existing masonry buildings, i.e. the Gothic Grodzka Tower, the Major Court and the former residence of Sigismundus Augustus were preserved (in accordance with the King's wishes) and new three-storey wings were added to them from the north, west and south. A high, helmeted tower called the Sigismundus' or Clock Tower (from the large clock placed there in 1622) was built on the axis of the western wing and dominated the whole castle. In order to balance the excessive horizontality of the ten metre western front, it was flanked with two small towers, which added vertical accents. Furthermore, a roofed passage was built through the kitchen court providing a direct link between the castle and the royal box in the Collegiate Church of St.

The Castle and Sigismundus' Column   The Castle at night

John. The construction was undertaken after an attempt on Sigismundus III's life in 1620 made by the nobleman Michał Piekarski, when the king accompanied by his court was on his way to Sunday Mass.

The design for the extension of the castle was probably made by the King's architect Giovanni Trevano, and the construction was supervised first by Jacopo Rotondo and then by Matteo Castelli.

Ladislaus IV, Sigismundus' son and successsor, did not introduce many changes to the castle. The staircase tower in the bend of the north-eastern wing, which was named after Ladislaus, obtained a new, Baroque form and a Baroque helmet; it was probably planned by the royal architect, Constantino Tencalla. On the King's initiative, a monument to his father, Sigismundus III was erected near the western front of the castle.

Sigismundus III and then both his sons, Ladislaus and his brother and successor, Jan Kazimierz, were interested in art. All of them brought pictures from Italy and the Netherlands as well as collected artistic tapestries — arrases and Eastern carpets. In Sigismundus III's times, troupes of English comedians acted out the dramas of Shakespeare and Marlowe. Ladislaus IV organized a permanent theatre, where professional actors were employed.

The Swedish invasion of 1655 changed the fortune of the castle. It was robbed and demolished, while its art collections were scattered; many of the works were taken to Sweden.

The next stage in the history of the castle and its extensions is marked by the times of the kings from the Saxon dynasty. King Augustus II commissioned the transfer of the Seym Deputy Room from the ground floor of the Major Court to the first floor in the south-western corner of the castle. Also the Senate Room was rebuilt and a separate Throne Room was set up in one of the royal residential chambers in the north-eastern wing.

More construction work was undertaken under the reign of Augustus III. Between 1741—1746 the north-eastern wing was extended and from the Vistula side it was given a new, monumental, rococo façade with three projecting bays designed by Gaetano Chiaveri; the middle bay contained the great Audition Hall, while the ones at the sides housed the King's bedroom and a chapel. Antonio Solari was in charge of the construction work, while the sculptured ornaments were made by Jan Jerzy Plersch's workshop. In the subsequent years the so-called Great Outhouse was erected at the foot of the Castle — a long one story house containing accommodation for servants and storehouses. In the first half of the 19th century, the outbuilding was hidden behind a monumental arcaded terrace designed by Jakub Kubicki.

The last great reconstruction of the castle was conducted by Stanislaus Augustus. The work was supervised first by Jakub Fontana (until 1773) and then by Dominik Merlini. Large scale designs for changing the external appearance and surroundings of the castle made by Fontana and an

7

The Castle — the Sigismundus' Clock Tower

The Castle — Ladislaus' Tower

The Castle — eastern wall

architect brought from France, Victor Louis, which included an imposing colonnaded courtyard, were not carried out. Castle interiors, were, however, thoroughly changed, adjusted to their functions living chambers as well as rooms designed for official use and given a classicist form. Between 1780—1784 a new wing planned by Dominik Merlini with a large 56 metre long room designed to house the King's library was added. Pairs of Ionic columns divided the interior of the room into three parts; book shelves were placed in arcaded niches while above — reliefs in oval medallions portrayed the symbols of those fields of knowledge which were represented in the book collection. The room was decorated with marble busts of *Pope Leo X*, *Caesar* and *Aleksander the Great*, as well as the seated statue of *Voltaire* — a plaster cast copy of Jean Antoine Hudon's work.

The Royal Castle was neglected after the partitions and its art collections were taken away. In 1918, after Poland regained its independence, thorough restoration work was undertaken, as a result of which the Renaissance rooms and those from the period of Stanislaus Augustus regained their original appearance; works of art which had been taken to Russia were recovered. Since 1926, when the castle became the seat of the President of the Republic it was the venue for official state celebrations.

On 17 September, 1939, Germans threw fire bombs on the castle; the roof over the Great Ballroom collapsed and the plafond by Bacciarelli burned. After the German army entered Warsaw, all the precious works: furniture, paintings, carpets, etc. were systematically taken to Germany. Castle and National Museum employees assisted by the inhabitants of Warsaw succeeded, however, in saving a considerable part ot the works of art from the castle as well as some architectural and decorative elements, by taking them to the Museum. After the 1944 Warsaw Uprising, the castle was blown up.

The decision of rebuilding it was made on January 20, 1971. It was reconstructed in its pre-1939 form. Original architectural designs and inventory drawings as well as photographs of the Royal Castle before 1939 were meticulously imitated. In the process of reconstruction, extensive use was made of designs and inventory drawings as well as photographs of the Royal Castle before 1939. Preserved wall fragments were incorporated into the restored building and elements of carpentry and stuccowork, which had been removed from the old castle and stored, were included in the decorations of the interiors. All the works of art which had been saved: furniture, pictures and handicrafts were put in their original places in the castle rooms.

The Castle — Senate Room | The Castle — a fragment of Jan Matejko's painting *The Constitution of 3 May, 1791*

INTERIORS
OF THE CASTLE

Not all of the interiors were reconstructed according to their state in 1939.

The **Senate Room** was rebuilt according to designs by Saxon architects — therefore its interior is similar to what it was when the 3rd May Constitution was passed. It is decorated with pairs of Corinthian pilasters and coats of arms of the Polish Kingdom and the Great Duchy of Lithuania, as well as of all the voivodships and territories of the Republic. It was in this room that one of the most significant documents in the history of Poland was passed: the 3 May Constitution. The event was commemorated on canvas by Jan Matejko in his painting for the Castle Deputy Rooms. He portrayed the moment, when after passing the "Government Bill" all the deputies walk in a solemn procession from the Royal Castle to sing *Te Deum* at St. John's Church. Full of enthusiasm, on their shoulders they carry the Speaker of the Seym, Stanisław Małachowski, who holds a card with the text of the Constitution in his hand; a banner with the coat of arms of the Republic can be seen in the background. Świętojańska Street is filled with a cheering crowd. The façade of the Royal Castle, where the May Constitution was drafted, elaborated and passed, is visible in the distance.

The group of interiors from the Stanislaus period dating from the years 1774—1785 and situated in the eastern wing of the Royal Castle deserves special attention. They were designed mainly by Dominik Merlini, but their character, as well as that of all the art that developed under royal patronage in this period was to a large extent determined by the taste and artistic predilections of the monarch himself; their style called the style of Stanislaus Augustus is a courtly variation of early Polish classicism.

The **Canaletto Room** (the **Senators' Antechamber**), which served the function of an antechamber for guests waiting for an audience with the kings, dates from the years 1776—1777. Its architecture is rather modest and was to serve only as the setting for pictures representing sights of Warsaw and Wilanów painted by the Italian townscapist Bernard Belotto called Canaletto. The twenty two pictures which are in the room were painted in the years 1770—1780; they portray the streets and squares of the Warsaw city centre as it was in Canaletto's days: Krakowskie Przedmieście, Długa, Miodowa, and Senatorska Streets; the New Town market square, Krasiński' Square with their palaces and churches, as well as the life going on in those places: the gentry, rich townspeople and the city poor, carriages and peasant carts, street vendors and an itinerant orchestra. The most extensive panorama of the city is presented in the *General View of Warsaw from the Praga side*, with the Royal Castle with its rococo façade dominating over it. The foreground of this picture, which was painted in 1770, presents the self-portrait of the

The Castle — Canaletto's Room
(view of the southern wall)

The Castle, Bernardo Belotto called Canaletto,
View of Krakowskie Przedmieście from the Sigismundus Column, 1767—1768

Krakowskie Przedmieście as seen from Sigismundus' Column today

artist standing at his easel. The opposite wall presents an equally large picture representing the *Election of Stanislaus Augustus in 1764*. Fortunately, all the pictures decorating this room were saved during World War II, so after the Royal Castle was rebuilt, they were put in their original places.

Thanks to the artist's outstanding precision, they also played a very important role when the capital was being rebuilt after the war, constituting priceless iconographic material for the reconstruction of Warsaw's monuments.

In Grodzka Tower, next to the Canaletto Room, there used to be a **chapel** consisting of a small rectangular nave and a rotunda-shaped chancel with eight Corinthian columns of green stucco and gilded capitals and bases supporting a coffered dome decorated with gilded rosettes; the walls and window bays were made of red stucco.

The Canaletto Room leads to the **Old Audience Room**. In 1777, this room served the function of a Throne Room. It was decorated with a plafond and overdoor by Marcello Bacciarelli. The overdoors represent allegories of the four universal virtues of a good monarch: *Fortitude*, expressed as Samson fighting with a lion; *Prudence* — where the discretion of old age is contrasted with the passion of youth; *Faith* — represented as a woman with a glass in her hand; and the most important of royal virtues — *Jus-*

tice — shown as a woman with scales symbolising impartiality and a sword representing power. These virtues were to ensure lasting peace in the country, which would, in turn, allow it to flourish and grow rich. The culmination of the idea was portrayed in the plafond picture representing *The Thriving of Art, Science, Agriculture and Commerce under the Rule of Peace*, pointing to the development of cultural and economic life under the rule of Stanislaus Augustus. The plafond, which was destroyed during the war, was meticulously restored during the reconstruction of the Royal Castle. In its composition it has a counterpart in the floor, which is made of different-coloured circles of parquet.

The Throne Room leads to the King's chambers: his bedroom, wardrobe, and study and then to a series of rooms of official character, i.e. the so-called **Great Apartment of the Royal Castle**, consisting of the following: the **Throne Room (New Audience Room)**, situated in the southern bay projection of the Saxon wing. Its interior has been reconstructed on the basis of photographs made before 1939. The walls are lined with red damask framed by gilded carved batten and decorated with large mirrors in golden frames. Opposite the window is the authentic throne designed by Jan Chrystian Kamsetzer, with coats of arms of the Republic and of the King. Unfortunately its setting

The Castle — mantlepiece clock from the Ball-room
with the figure of *Orpheus*, first quarter of the 19th century

The Castle — the figure of *Cronos* from the Knight Room,
Jakub Monaldi, 1784—1786

The Castle — table with a porcelain top
from the Conference Cabinet, 1777

The Castle — Stanislaus Augustus' Chapel
On the following pages: The Castle — former Audience Room
The Castle — the Cabinet of European Monarchs
(Conference Cabinet)

was not preserved — originally the back and canopy were
decorated with silver embroidered eagles in golden
crowns. On the mantlepiece there are four marble copies
of ancient sculpture made in Rome in 1786. They portray
Scipio, Hannibal, Pompey and *Caesar* representing royal
virtues: *Temperance, Justice* and *Wisdom*.
A small octagonal room is connected to the Throne Room,
the so-called **Study of European Soverigns (Conference
Room)**, which Stanislaus Augustus dedicated to the European monarchs of his times. It is decorated with the portraits of: *Pope Pius VI* (over the door leading to the Throne Room), the *Emperess Catherine II* (over the fireplace),
the *Emperor Joseph II* (over the mirror niche), the
Gustavus III, King of Sweden (next to *Catherine II*, near
the door), *Louis XVI*, the King of France (opposite *Frede-
rick II*) and *George III*, the King of England (opposite
Gustavus III, near the door.) The portraits, in frames

The Castle Knight Room

crowned with the coats of arms of appropriate countries, have been incorporated into grotesque-arabesque decorations painted on a golden background by Jan Bogumił Plersch. The beautiful, many-coloured floor with patterned marquetry is an additional decorative element. Also the small table with a round inlaid top made in 1777 at a Serves workshop is part of the original furnishing of the Study. The table top is the work of the outstanding porcelain painter Charles Nicolas Dodin. The decoration tells the story of Telemachus, the son of Odysseus; the scenes are illustrations for *Les Aventures de Telemach*, written in 1699 by François Fenelon, which were so popular at the time.

The **Knights' Room** (the **Senators' Antechamber**) served the role of antechamber for people awaiting an audience. According to the King's intention it was to be a room commemorating the most glorious events in the history of Poland and the country's most distinguished people: leaders, statesmen, scientists and artists. This idea is clearly stated by a quotation from Vergil's *Aeneid* inscribed around the room in Latin. Translated, it means: "This is a host of those who suffered wounds for the fatherland, and those who led the clean life of priesthood, and those pious poets whose songs were worthy of Phoebus. And also those who creating the arts made life more beautiful, and those who thanks to their merits became immortalized in people's memories".

The room is decorated with six large historical canvases by Bacciarelli representing: the *Relief of the Siege of Vienna*, the *Chocim Peace Treaty*, the *Union of Lublin*, the *Prussian Homage*, *Awarding Privileges to the Cracow Academy*, the *Laws of Casimir the Great*. The ideas for these pictures came from Stanislaus Augustus. Besides, ten oval portraits of famous Poles, also by Bacciarelli, were placed in the overdoors. Each of the portraits was enclosed in a stucco frame with attributes due to the person represented by virtue of position, function or profession. The gallery of outstanding Poles is completed by twenty two bronze busts of leaders, statesmen, scientists and poets — made by the sculptors André Le Brun and Jakub Monaldi. The King commissioned the creation of such an extraordinary room, dedicated to the memory of the greatest people in the history of Poland, in order to arouse the spirit of patriotism and transmit the idea of the imperishability of great deeds and triumphs. He hoped it would awaken the need for the rebirth of old virtues which would help to establish peace leading to order and happiness.

This ideological programme is completed with two marble statues: that of *Cronos* presented as an old man with a scythe in his hand and carrying a star spangled globe (with built-in clock-work) upon his shoulders — the work of Monaldi, as well as *Fame* in the shape of a woman with a trombone in one hand and a golden crown in the other — made by Le Brun.

Adjacent to the Knights' Room is the **Marble Room**. This room, having walls lined with many-coloured marble, was furnished during the reign of Ladislaus IV according to designs by Gaetano Gisleni. Originally it was decorated with a plafond painted by Tomasz Dolabella, representing the coronation of Sigismundus III and a gallery of portraits of the Polish kings. Later neglected, it survived until Stanislaus Augustus' times in a very bad shape. In the years 1768–1771 it was renovated and rebuilt according to Jakub Fontana's designs. The lower part of the walls below the entablature and the door frame was left without any considerable changes. Also the ideological concept of the interior was left unchanged: Stanislaus Augustus, similarly to Ladislaus IV decided to dedicate the Study to the memory of his predecessors on the Polish throne. On the frieze over the cornice there are twenty two oval and rectangular portraits of Polish kings painted by Marcello Bacciarelli. The figures of those whose services for the country the King valued most, i.e. *Casimir the Great, Ladislaus Jagiełło, Sigismundus the Old, Ladislaus IV* and *Jan III*, were marked off by a richer setting. The full *Portrait of Stanislaus Augustus in coronation robes* was put over the fireplace, in a particularly notable part of the room. The opposite wall, under the cornice, was decorated with personifications of *Peace* and *Justice* holding a cartouche with the coats of arms of the Republic and of the King, carved in marble by Le Brun. The plafond, which was painted by Bacciarelli, represented *Fame announcing the deeds of Polish monarchs*.

This interior survived until 1835, when the marble walls were pulled down on the tsar's orders. Bacciarelli's plafond was demolished during World War II. The present reconstruction was made on the basis of Jan Chrystian Kamsetzer's water colour pictures representing the appearance of the Study in 1784.

The **Ball-room** (the **Assembly Room**) is the largest and most elegant among castle rooms. This double-storey Ball--room was established in the middle bay projection of the Saxon façade, in place of the former Audience Room of Augustus II's times. Its walls are divided by pairs of Corinthian stucco columns. The arcaded windows have their counterparts in the mirror niches on the opposite wall. On the axis of the room there is a great, vaulted semi-dome entrance niche with rosettes. The sculptured framework of the entrance is the work of André Le Brun. A bust of *Stanislaus Augustus* in profile was placed in the marble medallion in the overdoor, between winged figures personifying *Peace* and *Justice*. The entrance is flanked with two marble statues: that of *Stanislaus Augustus as Apollo with a lyre and a crown of laurels* and *Catherine II as Minerva*. The plafond by Marcello Bacciarelli represented the *Separation of the four elements* (*Jove leading the world out of chaos*). The original was destroyed when the Royal Castle was bombed in September, 1939. The present plafond was reconstructed by art restorers on the basis of Bacciarelli's sketches.

The Castle — Marble Room

On the following pages: The Castle — Ball-room

Castle Square — outlet of Piwna Street

CASTLE SQUARE

The square in front of the Royal Castle has the shape of an irregular triangle, from the east limited by the castle, from the north-west by the Old Town houses and from the south open towards Krakowskie Przedmieście. In the 14th century the place was occupied by defense walls linked with castle fortifications and the Cracow Gate, with the main road to Warsaw leading through it. Over subsequent centuries residential houses and the castle housekeeping court with stables, coach-houses, etc. (the so--called Front Courtyard) were built on the site. A church and Bernardine convent were situated between the Royal Castle and the Bernardine Church (St. Anne's Church). All this gradually accumulating architecture was disorderly and chaotic. In 1644, on the occasion of erecting the Sigismundus' column, part of the site was cleared. It was only in the 19th century, however, that the square was eventually redesigned by the architect Jakub Kubicki. The Cracow Gate, and the buildings of the Front Courtyard,

as well as several houses, were demolished. As a result, the area around the western front of the Royal Castle with the Sigismundus tower was cleared, so both became clearly visible. In 1843 the buildings of the church and Bernardine convent were pulled down and between 1844—1846 a viaduct designed by the outstanding constructor Feliks Pancer and constituting a downhill road to the Powiśle district was built between St. Anne's Bell Tower and the Pod Blachą Palace (Under the Tin Roof Palace). Now the W—Z Thoroughfare (East—West Thoroughfare), which was built after World War II runs in place of the former viaduct. The eastern part of the square is closed by a stone balustrade, with a view extending over the Vistula and right bank Warsaw. The Baroque Under the Tin Roof Palace with two late Baroque outbuildings is situated at the southern wing of the Castle. It was erected at the beginning of the 18th century for Deputy Chancellor Jerzy Dominik Lubomirski. During the reign of Stanislaus Augustus, the palace belonged to his nephew, Prince Józef Poniatowski.

SIGISMUNDUS' COLUMN

The centre of the Castle Square is dominated by the Sigismundus' Column, probably the best known monument in the city. It is so closely associated with Warsaw that it became its visiting card, its second, unofficial coat of arms. The column is the oldest monument not only in Warsaw, but in all of Poland. It was erected in 1644, commissioned by King Ladislaus IV, who in this way wanted to pay tribute to his father. The Latin inscriptions on the bronze plaques affixed to the four sides of the base are a sort of panegyric to Sigismundus III: they acclaim the fame, greatness and merits of the deceased, at the same time adding to the prestige of Ladislaus IV as his son and successor to the Polish throne. Besides filial affection, the latter reason — i.e. the wish to underline the importance of the royal Vasa dynasty — constituted significant motivation to erect such an imposing monument, situated in such a universally accessible place (near the Royal Castle, opposite the Cracow Gate, which was the main entrance to Warsaw). Using the column form also had a symbolic role referring to ancient Roman tradition (cf. Trajan's Column erected in 113 A.D. or Marcus Aurelius' Column from 176 – 193), when the column played the function of glorifying a leader and ruler and was to commemorate his martial feats and proclaim his glory.

The Warsaw monument is 22 metres high and consists of three parts: a double base with a slender Corinthian column — on which in turn there is quite a high pedestal — and the bronze gilded statue of Sigismundus III. The monument as a whole was designed by the architect Konstanty Tencalli. The Italian sculptor Clemente Molli was the author of the model for the King's figure, while the bronze mould was made by Daniel Tym. The statue was cast in one part. The King's face shows remarkable similarly to all his extant portraits. He is dressed in archaized armour and the royal robe, which is thrust back on both sides and does not obscure the figure, but constitues a sort background. On his head he has a crown and in his hands he holds a sword and a cross — attributes of a ruler being also a defendant of faith. The statue was specially adapted to the place where it would stand; the figure is elongated, especially in the legs, which was to offset its shortening when seen in perspective from below. Besides a symbolic meaning, the column form applied to Sigismundus III's statue had a purely practical function. At the time it was being erected, the site around it was densely and chaotically built up; the small square made for the statue was surrounded by both monumental buildings and one-storey houses, stables, etc. Placing the column of the King on a tall column towering over its surroundings, made the silhouette stand out against the sky and clearly visible from a distance, ensuring the view was not obstructed by near-by buildings.

Castle Square with Sigismundus' Column

On the following pages: Sigismundus' Column

Piwna Street

Świętojańska Street

Fragment of an Old Town house

OLD TOWN

Situated north-west of the Royal Castle, within the framework of the defence walls, the Old Town constituted the embryo of present-day Warsaw. It was set up at the turn of the thirteenth and fourteenth century, when the Mazowsze Dukes left their castle in Jazdów and transferred their seat to the later site of the Royal Castle. At the turn of the fourteenth and fifteenth century the New Town was established north of the Old Town. Typically for this period, the urban grid of the Old Town is that of the chessboard. The market square is a rectangle with two streets starting at every corner. Construction sites were set out perpendicularly to the street grid. The Warsaw Old Town has a characteristic feature in being situated a little to the side — probably due to the existence of an earlier settlement, which was later adapted to the town arrangement. Already in the Middle Ages masonry houses with arched windows, portals, niches and polychromed interiors were built here. Over the next centuries, this architecture underwent considerable changes, first brought about in the seventeenth century. During the Swedish wars, much of Warsaw was destroyed and its buildings suffered a lot. In the course of reconstruction, an effort was made

to "modernise" the houses, redecorating them according to current artistic trends. Many Old Town buildings were then given Baroque fronts, but the centre of town life began moving beyond Old Town walls. The process, which continued over the 18th and 19th centuries, resulted in the Old Town becoming a poor, overpopulated peripheral district full of small shops and workshops; its housing gradually deteriorated. In order to save the historical houses from ruin, action was initiated by the Society for the Protection of Historical Monuments which was organized in 1906. It was on its initiative that façades of houses in the market place were renovated in the inter-war period. During the Warsaw Uprising, for a month the Old Town was the scene of fierce, bloody fighting. The district was almost totally destroyed, and the remaining houses were blown up by the Germans after the insurgents had left the Old Town. Reconstruction was begun soon after the war. Despite the enormous scope of destruction, many elements of the architecture were saved. Fragments of portals or window frames found among the rubble were later used in reconstruction. Rebuilding of the Old Town was not limited to only one, chosen historical epoch. Efforts were made to uncover all the subsequent stages of the district's development. The Medieval urban system was maintained, keeping to the old street grid. It was not possible, however, to reconstruct the original, Gothic architecture, both due to the small number of extant relics and to inadequate iconographic materials. Restoration was based on materials from the 17th and 18th centuries. They mostly have Baroque, or — to a lesser extent — late Renaissance features. The historical height of the houses was preserved, and their external outline reconstructed, with the characteristic staircase lanterns extending over the roof-tops. Façades were decorated with polychromy appropriate for their architectural style. Sometimes the internal organization of the space in the houses had to be sacrificed in order to adapt them to the requirements of modern residential housing. Such decisions were, however, always subject to the degree of authenticity and the historical value of each house. Space on the ground floor was for most part taken over by shops, services, cafés and restaurants catering for the needs of both the district and the tourists visiting the Old Town. Such an arrangement followed the 19th century tradition, where ground floors of houses were mostly occupied by shops and craftsmen's workshops. The reconstructed Old Town now constitutes one of the beautiful historical districts of the Polish capital. In 1981 the UNESCO International Committee of World Heritage included Warsaw's historical centre on the list of Monuments of World Heritage.

OLD TOWN MARKET-PLACE

The Old Town Market-place was the heart of economic, social and political life of Old Warsaw. The first brick and masonry buildings in this area date from the 14th and 15th centuries. In the 15th century a Town-Hall was also erected here (it was pulled down in 1817). Houses around the Market-place belonged to the most outstanding patrician burgher families holding the highest posts in the Town Council and sometimes also at the royal court. In the 17th century most of these houses were reconstructed in Late Renaissance and Baroque styles. Superstructures over the roofs containing so-called lanterns providing light for staircases date from this period. In the 18th century most of the houses were extended upwards and some were given new fronts. The gradual degradation of the Old Town in the 19th century led to the loss of their former splendour. It was only in the 20th century that they were partly renovated. In the inter-war period the fronts were polychromed. Post-war reconstruction restored their late Renaissance or Baroque appearance.

In 1915 each side of the Market-place was named after people who rendered special services for Warsaw — city Presidents, active at the time of the Four-Year Seym and the Kościuszko Insurrection: Dekert, Brass and Zakrzew-

Old Town Market-place

View of the Market-place from Świętojańska Street

Clock on a house at the corner of the Market-place

„Little Negro House" — part of the wall

ski; as well as Hugo Kołłątaj, who was one of the most outstanding figures of the Polish Enlightenment.

Among the houses surrounding the Market-place, special attention should be paid e.g. to the one situated at the corner of Wąski Dunaj Street, called "St. Anne's House", named after the 16th century figure placed in its corner niche, which represents *St. Anne with the Blessed Virgin Mary and the Holy Infant*. Sometimes the house is also called the Mazowsze Dukes' House — although there is no justification for this name. Erected in the 14th century and reconstructed several times, it has maintained many of its original elements: the arched Gothic niches in the Wąski Dunaj Street front, two sixteenth century portals in the entrance hall, *St. Anne's* figure. The façade with a late Renaissance portal and sgraffito decoration comes from the first half of the 17th century; also the bay window dates from the same time. This building as well as the neighbouring one is the seat of the Polish Academy of Sciences History Institute. On the same side of the Market-place (i.e. Kołłątaj's side) at number 27 is the Fukier House with a cloister in the inner courtyard. Erected in the middle of the 16th century in place of an earlier house, reconstructed in the 17th and 18th century, since 1810 it belonged to Marcin Fukier, who established his famous wine cellar here. Between 1910—1920 it was restored

under the supervision of Władysław Marconi. During post-war reconstruction, the façade was given a classicist decoration. Now it houses the Art Historians' Association and the Union of Polish Composers.

The "Pod Murzynkiem" (Little Negro) house situated in the northern frontage of the Market-place (Dekert's side) called so from the sculpture representing a Negro's head, has a beautiful late Renaissance façade. It was erected in the second half of the 17th century for Mayor Jakub Dzianotti. The portal and window frames as well as the sgrafitto façade decoration come from this period. Interiors of the buildings on the Dekert side were adapted to house the Historical Museum of Warsaw. Exhibitions in the Museum present the history of Warsaw: its social, political and cultural life since the beginnings to the present--day. Besides documents, seals, maps and plans there are also handicrafts, pictures and sculptures from various periods, which are works by Warsaw artists or have thematic links with the capital city. The Warsaw Old Town Market-place has its own, unique atmosphere, which is created by the charm and beauty of the old houses which surround it, as well as by the colourful umbrellas stretched over the tables in outdoor cafés, the flower and souvenir stalls, and the pictures exhibited by students of the Academy of Fine Arts constituting a real open air gallery.

The Barbican

CITY WALLS

The original fortifications of the Old Town consisted of an earlier bailey raised from the north, the west and the south. Over the 14th and 15th centuries the bailey was gradually substituted by a brick wall with towers and gates, which provided more secure protection for the city. Over the 16th century the north side was additionally strengthened by an external wall with rectangular towers covered with high brick helmets and the **Barbican** built in 1548 according to the design by Jan Baptysta, the Italian architect from Venice who worked in the Mazowsze region. The huge, semi-circular building with loopholes and a Renaissance Polish parapet consisting of alternating pinnacles and pyramids protected access to the town from the north. The Barbican had an entrance gate with a drawbridge; it was flanked with semi-circular towers supported by rectangular pillars.

·During the many wars waged in the 17th and at the begin-

ning of the 18th century the walls were repeatedly damaged. In the latter 18th and in the 19th century they were partly removed and partly absorbed by the developing city architecture — such was e.g. the fortune of the Barbican. In the 19th century several city gates were pulled down (including the Cracow Gate near the Royal Castle, through which the main road to Warsaw from the south used to lead, as well as the lookout tower on the Vistula side, the so-called Marshall Tower — Wieża Marszałkowska). In the inter-war period, between 1937—1938, parts of the city walls and the moat near the Barbican as well as the Barbican bridge, were reconstructed and unveiled. When some 18th and 19th century houses in Podwale Street burnt down in 1944, long stretches of city walls, hitherto hidden in the dense housing, were uncovered. Between 1953—1963 both lines of the walls with towers and the Barbican were partly reconstructed. Throughout the summer the region is a venue for individual exhibitions by Warsaw artists.

Mermaid statue on Old Town walls

MERMAID MONUMENT

The *Mermaid Monument* standing on the walls of the Old Town, where the Marshall Tower used to stand, is a zinc cast of the sculpture by Konstanty Hegel, made in 1855. In the inter-war period it was a decoration of the Old Town Market-place and it has been in its present place since 1972.

The Mermaid figure with a shield in one hand and a raised sword in the other, is featured in Warsaw's coat of arms and has become the symbol of the city. The image underwent different metamorphoses over the centuries. In the oldest, fifteenth century representations on seals, the Warsaw coat of arms is depicted as a winged monster armed with a sword and shield. It had the body of a man, the legs of a bull and a lion's tail. In the middle of the sixteenth century the Mermaid had features of a woman, but it did not lose its monstrous characteristics: it was a creature with a dragon's wings, with claws and the tail of a reptile and thighs covered with fish scales. In this form it survived until the 18th century, when under the influence of classicist trends, the medieval monster was replaced by a shapely woman with a curled up fish tail in place of legs, holding a shield and a sword raised over her head. The figure was probably formed under the influence of antique representations of water gods and goddesses, i.e. Poseidon's attendants, the Tritons, or representations of the beautiful sorceress from a French legend called Melusina — half woman, half snake. In its present shape the capital's coat of arms was approved in 1939.

32

STATUE OF JAN KILIŃSKI

Kiliński was a Warsaw shoemaker, who during the Warsaw Insurrection stood at the head of Old Town folk and conquered the seat of the Czar's ambassador Ingelström in Podwale Street. Nominated colonel by Tadeusz Kościuszko, he fought in defense of Warsaw, and was twice wounded. After the fall of the insurrection he was arrested, extradited to Russian officials and then sent for several years to a tower in St. Petersburg. In 1936 a monument made by Stanisław Jackowski was erected in Warsaw to honour the heroic shoemaker. Originally it stood in Krasińskis' Square, in front of the palace. During the war, in 1942, the Germans removed the statue, transferring it in secret to the National Museum. This was done in revenge for taking off a German tablet from the statue of Copernicus and unveiling a Polish one. A few days after the statue of *Kiliński* was taken to the Museum, an inscription saying "People of Warsaw! I am here! Kiliński" appeared on its walls. The operation was part of the so-called small sabotage conducted by scouts from Szare Szeregi (Grey Squads). Besides, the following writing appeared on signposts: "In retaliation for demolishing the statue of *Kiliński* I order winter to last six weeks longer. Mikołaj Kopernik, astronomer".

In 1945, immediately after the war, the statue returned to its original place and in 1959 it was transferred to Podwale Street.

Monument to Jan Kiliński

Castle Square at night

View of the Castle from Kanonia Street

Piwna Street at night

ST. JOHN'S CATHEDRAL

This is the oldest church in Warsaw. The original, wooden edifice was replaced at the beginning of the fifteenth century by a masonry one, founded by Duke Janusz the Elder. In the 17th century it gained a new façade, in the 19th century it was thoroughly rebuilt by Adam Idźkowski in the style of the English Gothic. During the Warsaw Insurrection, the church, as one of the basic defense posts for the Old Town region, was practically levelled. After the war it was rebuilt in the so-called Vistula Gothic style.
The interior of the church is a three naved hall (all the naves are of equal height) with a prolonged closed trian-

St. John's Cathedral — interior

Church of the Blessed Virgin Mary in the New Town
— view from the Vistula River bank

gular chancel. Special attention should be paid to the late Gothic so-called *Baryczkowski Crucifix* made in the early 16th century. According to tradition, it was brought from Nurnberg by the Warsaw councillor Jerzy Baryczka. The figure of the crucified Christ is remarkable for its expressiveness. The face conveys boundless pain and suffering. The *Crucifix* is placed in Jesus the Miraculous Chapel (Baryczków Chapel).

Another special feature of the church is the tombstone of the last Mazowsze Dukes: Stanisław (d. 1524) and Janusz (d. 1525) made between 1527—1528 of red Chęcin marble. It was made by the Italian sculptor Bernardino Zanobi de Gianotis. Also the statue of *Stanisław Małachowski*, the Marshall of the Four-Year Seym, deserves attention. It was made in 1831 following the design of the Danish sculptor, Bertel Thorvaldsen.

NEW TOWN

CHURCH OF THE VISITATION

The Church of the Visitation was founded in 1409 by Duke Janusz the Elder and his wife Anneas to serve as the parish church for the New Town located north of the Old Town. This small one nave church with a polygonal closed chancel was enlarged in the second half of the 15th century and changed into a basilica, with buttresses on the outside and crowned with stepped gables. In 1518 the southern nave was extended by a slender bell tower with an arched passage on the ground level, also crowned with a stepped gable. In the 17th and 18th century two Baroque chapels were erected on both sides of the chancel. The exquisite style of the church was somewhat lost in the later restructuring work. Between 1906—1915 its Gothic character was restored under the supervision of Józef Pius Dziekoński and Stefan Szyller. Burned during the Warsaw Insurrection, the church was rebuilt in Gothic forms in the years 1947—1952. With its slender belfry the church is a beautiful landmark in the New Town panorama.

SACRAMENTINES' CHURCH

The church of the Sisters of the Blessed Sacrament under the vocation of St. Casimir is situated in the eastern part of New Town Market-place. The Sacramentines, i.e. Benedictine Sisters of the Unceasing Adoration of the Holy Sacrament, were brought from France in 1687 by Queen Maria Kazimiera Sobieska. She also founded a church and convent for them in Warsaw. Her foundation is traditionally referred to as the Queen's vow, reportedly made a day before King Jan III relieved the siege of Vienna. Planning the church was entrusted to the outstanding architect of Dutch descent, Tylman of Gameren. The resulting building is constructed as a Greek cross with an octagonal middle part covered by a dome. The lower part of the building, with clearly set out arms of the cross crowned by triangular gables decorated with the coat of arms cartouches and monograms of the founder, was divided by Tuscan pilasters on high pedestals. The compact and harmonious corpus of the temple is remarkable for its slenderness and elegance of proportions, while the decoration is characterized by serenity, elegance and a classical temperance. The church outline has been compared to a tabernacle in the shape of a *tempieto* (a small centralized church); such a form of the buildings was to be associated with the ideological premises of the congregation, devoted to the Perpetual Adoration of the Holy Sacrament. The slender, lit up interior of the church constitutes a uniform and harmonious whole. The shallow, one bay arms of the cross, covered with a barrel vault encompassing the main altar and the musical choir and side altars, were subordinated to the central nave, over which extends the dome on a high drum. The many windows which were pierced through it, let in light, modelling and enlivening the walls. In the middle of the 18th century the tomb of King Jan III's granddaughter, Maria Karolina née Sobieska, Duchess de Bouillon, was placed in the interior. The tomb, with a large arcade, sarcophagus and allegoric female figure, was the work of the Italian sculptor, Lorenzo Matella. The Sacramentines' Church together with the convent attached to it was altogether destroyed in the Warsaw Insurrection of 1944. Since the first days of the Insurrection nuns gave refuge to the nearby civilians in church and convent cellars. In August a hospital for insurgents was also set up. Due to the exceptional nature of the situation, the sisters decided to break the strict enclosure, which is one of the basic tenets of their congregation, and gave up their rooms to wounded insurgents. In retaliation, Germans bombed both the church and the convent, practically levelling them. After the war, in the years 1949—1953 the church was rebuilt; between 1960—1961 also the tomb of Karolina de Bouillon was reconstructed.

New Town Market-place with the Sacramentines' Church   Sacramentines' Church and convent

KRAKOWSKIE PRZEDMIEŚCIE

Krakowskie Przedmieście (the Cracow Suburb) runs south from the Castle Square. It is the road leading from the former Cracow Gate to Ujazdów and further on to Czersk — the main southward route from the old Warsaw. Until the 15th century it used to be called the Czerskie Przedmieście, and after the erection of the Bernardine church and monastery — the Bernardyńskie Przedmieście. Its present name gained acceptance around the middle of the 16th century. Over the 17th and 18th centuries, many magnificent magnate residences and burgher houses as well as churches were built here. The street became one of the most elegant arteries of the capital.

In the part of Krakowskie Przedmieście between the Castle Square and Miodowa (Honey) Street, opposite St. An-

Prażmowskis' house — fragment of the wall

Row of houses in Krakowskie Przedmieście

John's house — part of the wall facing Castle Square

ne's Church, there is a series of exceptionally interesting 18th century burgher houses. The so-called John's house (from the name of one of its owners, Aleksander John) which is closest to the Square, was built in the middle of the 18th century. It is covered by a high mansard roof, the fronts of which are decorated with flat lesenes; the upper part of the walls and the panels placed between windows on each story is decorated with delicate rococo ornaments. The house, destroyed during the last war, was reconstructed on the basis of Canaletto's picture representing the view of Krakowskie Przedmieście as seen from the Sigismundus' Column. The neighbouring Prażmowskis' house is probably one of the finest examples of Rococo burgher houses. Erected between 1660—1667 for the royal doctor, Pastorius, it was then the property of Mikołaj Prażmowski. In 1754 it was thoroughly reconstructed in Late Baroque style for the Leszczyńskis' family. The Krakowskie Przedmieście façade with a rococo decoration is flat at the sides and somewhat concave on the axis; it is

crowned by a rococo cartouche. A further decorative element are the quartercircular balconies placed on three stories along the middle axis and surrounded by cast iron balustrades. The Senatorska Street front has a classicist decoration, which was made at the end of the 18th century. In the 19th century two axes of the neighbouring building were linked to the house. Now it is the seat of the Polish Writers' Union.

At the corner of Miodowa Street rises the monumental, classicist house built in 1784 according to Szymon Bogumił Zug's design for the co-owners of a commercial company, the merchants Roessler and Hurtig. On the ground floor it housed a big department store, while the first floor was occupied by flats and the owners' apartments. Towards the end of the 19th century it was enlarged by an extra wing. The side front, which emerged after the opening of Miodowa Street, was then also designed. Roessler and Hurtig's house was the first large department store in Warsaw.

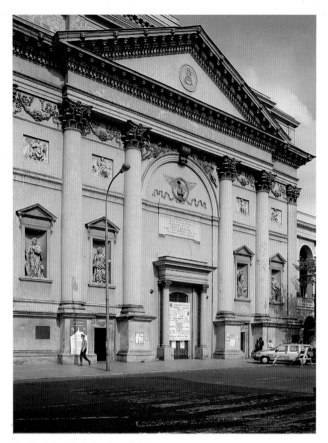

St. Anne's Church — façade

St. Anne's Church — view of the chancel

St. Anne's Church — interior

ST. ANNE'S CHURCH

Situated very picturesquely on the high Vistula slope, St. Anne's Church is exceptionally interesting both from the historical and architectural point of view. Built and extended for over three centuries, it bears clear stylistic marks of subsequent periods. The body of the church reflects the phases of its history: the low apse constitutes the remainder of the first church, the adjacent higher chancel and the even higher corpus church come from later periods. In general, the present church and its interior are Baroque, but fragments of Gothic walls can be found in the chancel area. The chapel of the Krycki family adjacent to the northern side (now it is the Ladyslaw of Gielniów Chapel) was built in late Renaissance style, while the façade is classicist in style.

The church was erected in 1454 and founded by the Mazowsze Duches Anne and her son Bolesław IV for the Bernardine monks, who had been brought to Poland (originally to Cracow), only a year before. It was a brick church, built on the plan of an elongated rectangle, closed from three sides in the east. The Gothic walls of the pre-

sent-day chancel are relicts of this first church. As its patron, the church received the founder of the order, St. Bernard of Siena (the dedication to St. Anne emerged only in the 16th century). In 1515 the church burned, and rebuilding work as well as extension work was begun. This stage lasted eighteen years, until 1533. The remainder of the second church is the red brick northern part of the corpus wall of today's church with the now blocked up pointed arch windows. Between 1578—1584 a belfry founded by Queen Anna Jagiellonka was built next to the church. In 1620 a four sided chapel with a dome then fulfilling the role of the mausoleum of the Kryskis family from Drobin was built by the northern wall of the chancel. During the Swedish siege of Warsaw in 1657, the church burned down. Rebuilding was started already the following year and work lasted until 1667. The hitherto Gothic church was then given a Baroque architectural form, maintaining the original construction walls. The church was heightened, the pointed arch windows blocked up, new rectangular windows were broken through, and a second row of square windows was added in the superimposed nave and chancel area. The date of finishing con-

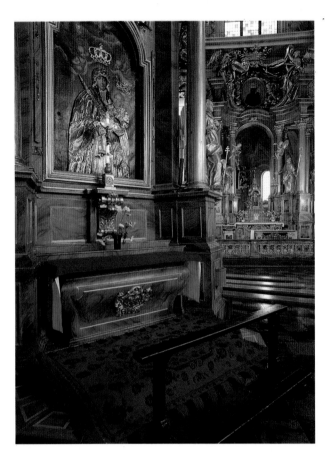

On this and the following page:
St. Anne's Church — interior

struction, A.D. MDCLXVII, was featured on the eastern wall of the church.

The last change in the external appearance of the church took place in the years 1786—1788, when a new classicist façade replaced the Baroque one. Some old elements were either taken away or covered up, while others were given new forms, originating from motifs dating from ancient Roman architecture, such as the Corinthian portico or the arch of triumph. The church was modelled after the façades of two Venetian churches — II Redentore (the Redeemer's) and San Giorgio Maggiore (St. George's), erected by the outstanding Renaissance architect Andrea Palladio (1508—1588). The plan for the Warsaw façade resulted from the cooperation of the architect Piotr Aigner and Stanisław Kostka Potocki — the Polish Enlightenment activist and art connoisseur; it was founded by King Stanislaus Augustus and the burgher Józef Kwieciński. The façade is decorated with figures of the four *Evangelists* placed in rectangular niches carved by Jakub Monaldi (according to tradition, *St. John's* figure has the facial features of King Stanislaus Augustus). Over the main portal is the commemorative tablet informing about the main merits of the founder, the reigning monarch, and the time the work originated, and above it an eagle with spread wings and

a crown of laurels. Over the archivolt of the great arcade encompassing the portal are two winged personifications of *Fame*. The clock originally placed in the tympanum was in the 19th century replaced by the stucco monogram "SA", which can be read as Santa Anna, or — Stanislaus Augustus. In the south, a neoclassical arcaded colonnade is adjacent to the church, which was erected between 1819—1821, concealing the front of the convent's western wing. While building the colonnade, a new Neo-renaissance form was given to the belfry founded in the 16th century by Anna Jagiellonka and it was connected with the church by an arcaded wall, in this way making a stylistically harmonious whole. Both of these works were authored by Aigner.

The interior of the church, consistently Baroque in form, strikes by the magnificence of decorations and the wealth of equipment, mostly coming from the 17th and beginning of the 18th century. Architectural details of the interior have mature Baroque forms; the light reflected in windows imitating mirrors, which are placed in niches on the southern wall, increase the effect of movement and the dynamics of form by means of strong light and shade contrasts. The whole interior was covered with paintings made in the 1740's by brother Walenty Żebrowski. Under

44

the entablature there are painted cartouches with representations of prophets and prophetesses.

The chancel decorated with four large imitations of church niches, out of which two encompass portals, while illusionist altars with the picture of the *Holy Virgin adored by the Blessed Jan of Dukla* and *Rafał of Proszowice* were inscribed into the remaining two. There are also illusionist niches under each of the nave windows, while decorative panneaux with landscapes and architecture were painted on the pillars. The Angelic Blessed Virgin Mary was represented on the apse vault behind the altar, while in the chancel and nave vaults there are scenes from St. Anne's legend and the childhood of the Blessed Virgin Mary based on texts from the *Apocrypha* (all of these pictures are reconstructions). Between 1751—1753 Żebrowski also polychromed the chapel of the Blessed Ladyslaw of Gielniów (formely the Kryskis' chapel), who had been the patron saint of Poland, Lithuania and Warsaw. Over the portal leading to the chapel on the chancel side is the end of the 17th century figure of the winged *Fame* standing on the globe of the heavenly sphere. On the sides of the heavenly globe two *putti* hold the attribute of the Blessed Ladyslaw: the scourge, and Christ near the flagellation pole. The composition was made according to the plan by Tylman of Gameren. Tylman was probably also the author of the design for the main altar, which comes from the years 1677—1680. Taking the whole width of the chancel, the altar divides it into two parts: the higher Baro-que one and the lower apse (where the convent choir used to stand). It was composed of six spatially spread out Corinthian columns placed on double linked pedestals encompassing the great arcade; the arcade opens on to the picture placed at the back, on the wall of the apse representing *St. Anne with Maria, the Holy Infant and St. Joseph*. Figures of the saints of the Bernardine order stand between the columns. At the top of the altar there is an oval picture of the *Virgin Mary with the Holy Infant supported by two putti*. Most interesting and original is the decoration of the pedestals for which the technique of Chinese laques with oriental motifs was used. Exotic landscape, fantastic buildings, blooming tress and branches, birds of Paradise, flamingoes, ring doves, butterflies were used as themes of the representations. The six architectural side altars come from the first quarter of the 18th century. Besides altars, the furnishings of the church also include a pulpit decorated with sculpture of seated monks and crowned with the figure of the *Blessed Ladyslaw of Gielniów*, as well as an 18th century confessional with representations of *St. Peter* and *St. John Nepomucen*, for which the marquetry technique was used. It seems that none of the Warsaw churches has extant interior decoration of comparable class. Fortunately, St. Anne's church was not destroyed during the war; partly burned, it was meticulously restored in the years 1946—1962 and now fulfils the functions of the academic church devoted to preaching to college and university students.

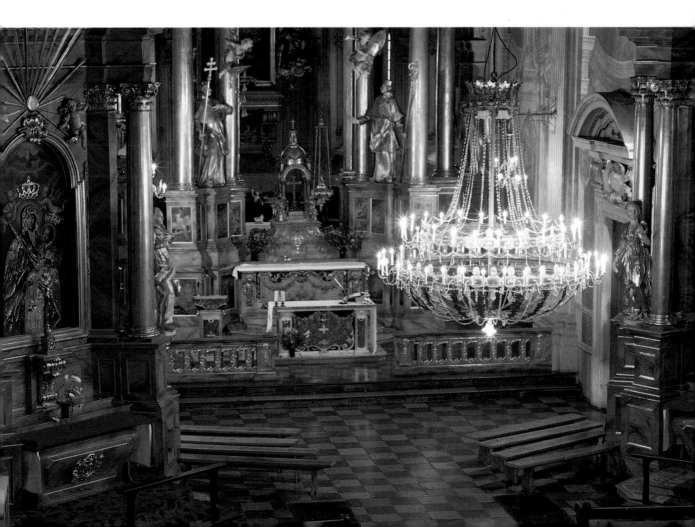

Figure of *Our Lady of Passau*

Monument to Adam Mickiewicz

FIGURE OF THE VIRGIN MARY OF PASSAU

Near the church of St. Anne stands the stone figure of the *Blessed Virgin Mary of Passau*. The small statue, which was fortunately untouched by historical upheavals, has unchangeably been standing in the small square near Krakowskie Przedmieście. The sculpture, which was finished in 1683, is the second one erected in Warsaw after Sigismundus III's Column. It was made by the architect Józef Szymon Belotti. The Madonna figure is a sculptural version of the Passau painting representing the *Blessed Virgin Mary with the Holy Infant* (from the Cranach circle), glorified in Eastern Europe as the protectress against pestilence. It seems, though, that the statue was not erected to protect against pestilence, but to commemorate King Jan III's victory near Vienna. Maria embraces the Infant in a gesture full of motherly affection, but looks over His head towards the city. The work bears marks of an experienced sculptor, who was able to overcome the difficulties emerging from its being set on quite a high pedestal; he consciously used some deformations of the figure's facial features to balance its perspective shortening while watching the figure from below and from the front.

MONUMENT TO ADAM MICKIEWICZ

The statue commemorating the figure of the great Polish national poet was erected from funds raised by public subscriptions of the Polish society on the hundredth anniversary of his birthday in 1898. Henryk Sienkiewicz, later a Nobel Prize laureate, was in charge of the committee which collected the money. The monument was executed by Cyprian Godebski, who came from a Polish family, although he permanently lived in France, where he was a highly esteemed artist with considerable achievements; i.e. he carved the busts of outstanding Poles — those of Konarski, Kraszewski, Mickiewicz, as well as compositions devoted to national topics, though all of those remained abroad.

Mickiewicz's statue was to be placed in the heart of Warsaw, in the very elegantly and centrally situated square near Krakowskie Przedmieście, next to the Carmelite church. In accordance with the wishes of the commissioning committee, it was to be simple, with the figure of the poet on a pedestal, unaccompanied by any allegorical figures or unnecessary symbols. The artist complied with these requirements. The statue is 14.5 metres in height, with the figure itself over 4 metres high. The poet was represented standing, dressed in his usual attire — a frock coat and overcoat on his shoulders; his eyes are raised in inspiration to the sky and his right hand is on his breast. The pedestal, executed according to plans by Józef Pius Dziekoński and Władysław Marconi is decorated with the head of Apollo — the god of art. The rays surrounding the head symbolize poetic inspiration. Three attributes of poetry: the lyre, palm branches and scrolls of papyrus are placed over Apollo's head. On the pedestal there is an engraved inscription: "To Adam Mickiewicz from his compatriots", as well as the date — 1898. The statue was universally praised for its realism, the resemblance to the poet and faithfulness in representing the costume, as well as the Romanticism expressed in the pose and gesture of the poet.

The ceremony of unveiling the statue took place on December 24, 1898.

CARMELITE CHURCH

The Carmelite Church dedicated to the Ascension of the Virgin Mary and St. Joseph, was built after the design by Józef Szymon Belotti. The interior is Baroque in form, while the façade, founded by Michał and Karol Radziwiłł, planned by Efraim Szreger between 1761—1762, is the earliest example of classical architecture in Poland. Construction was finished in 1782. The architect referred to the traditional 17th century scheme of the two story church façade, simplifying it and doing away with Baroque elements. Instead of groups of figures, he placed original, small belfries on either side of the building. The middle part is on both stories flanked with two double column porticoes, while the whole is crowned by a big copper ball, symbolizing the globe. The front of the church is one of the few in Warsaw made of ashlar. The classicist serenity and harmony of the architecture is somewhat disrupted by the sculptural decorations, which clearly have extant rococo features; this is visible especially in the allegorical figures of *Hope* and *Love* placed at the top, represented as women surrounded by groups of children.

The interior of the church consists of a nave with a transept and rows of side chapels connected both with the nave and each other by means of arcaded passages; the crossing of the naves was underlined by a blind dome, the walls are decorated with Corinthian pilasters. The main and side altars come from the mid 18th century. The left altar encompasses the sculptured group of *Espousals of Our Lady* by Jan Jerzy Plersch, also from the 18th century. In the altars of the chapels on the northern side, there are two paintings by Franciszek Szmuglewicz representing *St. Laurence* and *St. John of the Cross*.

Monument to Adam Mickiewicz and the Carmelites' Church

Wessels' Palace (building of the Saxon Post Office)

Wessels' Palace — part of the wall

Czartoryskis' Palace
(building of the Ministry of Culture and Art) — gate

WESSELS' PALACE (SAXON POST OFFICE)

The palace, erected about the mid 18th century for General Franciszek Jan Załuski is situated at the intersection of Kozia, Trębacka and Krakowskie Przedmieście Streets, alongside other buildings, and could be distinguished from burgher houses only by its scale and number of axes. The rich and at the same time delicate decoration of the front is maintained in rococo forms. Since 1761, the palace belonged to Theodore Wessel. Between 1780—1784 it was the seat of the royal post. Towards the end of the 19th century it was rebuilt after the designs of Władysław Marconi; it was then extended by an extra storey and a new front had to be built, due to the widening of Trębacka Street. Now the palace is the seat of the Head Office of the State Attorney.

CZARTORYSKIS' (POTOCKIS') PALACE

The former Warsaw residence of Maria and Augustus Czartoryski in Krakowskie Przedmieście is one of a group of elegant palaces built on the plan of a shoehorse, with side wings encompassing the court of honour separated from the street by a decorative fence. The layout was established in the 1730's when the 17th century palace, which formerly belonged to the Denhoff family, was extended. The greatest architects of the period — Józef Fontana and Jan Zygmunt Deybel — cooperated in erecting the new residence. In 1763 the guardhouse was erected in Krakowskie Przedmieście. It was maintained in Baroque forms, with sculptural decoration executed by Sebastian Zeisel. Towards the end of the 18th century, when the residence belonged to Duchess Izabela Lubomirska née Czartoryska, the main body of the palace was enriched by the classicist portico designed by Szymon Bogumił Zug; simultaneously work on rebuilding and decorating the interiors was carried out following the designs by Jan Chrystian Kamsetzer. In 1897, restoration work of the palace, which then already belonged to the Potocki family, was conducted under the supervision of Władysław Marconi. The beautiful iron gates with the Potockis' Pilawa coat of arms designed in Louis XV style by Marconi, come from the same period. Now the palace is the seat of the Ministry of Culture and Art, while the guardhouse is an art gallery where temporary exhibitions of Polish art are held.

Visitation Nuns' Church

VISITATION NUNS' CHURCH

The Visitation Nuns, or nuns belonging to the Order of the Visitation of the Blessed Virgin Mary were brought to Poland from Paris in 1654 by Louise Maria Gonzaga, wife of King Jan Kazimierz. The original church and convent founded by Louise Maria were wooden. The present church, dedicated to St. Joseph, was built in stages over the 18th century and is an outstanding example of Late Baroque church architecture in Poland. It was designed by Karol Bay and founded by Elżbieta Sieniawska, wife of the hetman. The first stage of construction fell on the years 1728—1733, when due to lack of funds the work had

to be interrupted. It was resumed only in the latter part of the century, in the years 1754—1763, under the supervision of an outstanding architect of that period, Efraim Szreger. Althout the church was erected in two phases with quite a long interval in between and built according to different artistic concepts, it constitutes a harmonious whole and the earlier and later parts complement each other very well. This can best be illustrated by the front, whose two lower stories were planned by Bay, while the cresting by another author — possibly Jakub Fontana. The lower part of the front has a plastic, multi-plan, seemingly undulating surface of the walls, divided by pairs of columns with niches and windows in between. The flat, almost linear cresting, with a surface divided by six Corinthian pilasters, presents a contrast to it, though no disharmony is introduced. The façade is decorated with figures placed in niches and on the cresting as well as with a Rococo ornament. In the niches of the middle storey there are figures of those who set the rule for the Visitation Nuns' order: *St. Francis de Sales* and *St. Augustine*. The symbol of Divine Providence (an eye in a triangle) was represented in the tympanum, and the Visitation scene in the niche of the cresting; next, on pedestals were placed figures of Maria's parents, *St. Anne* and *St. Joachim*, as well as *St. John the Baptist* and *St. Joseph*. On the top of the façade there is a cross adored by two angels.

The interior of the church has one nave with two rows of side chapels and a chancel which is slinghtly narrowed than the nave. The magnificent architectural main altar designed by Efraim Szreger and executed in Jan Plersch's workshop is crowned by the very expressive figure of *God the Father* seated in glory and blessing the faithful, accompanied by angels and *putti* as well as a she-dove — the

symbol of the Holy Ghost. In the altar is a painting by Tadeusz Kuntze-Konicz representing the scene of the *Visitation*, as well as a 17th century ebony tabernacle in the form of a Baroque church front founded by Queen Louise Maria.

The boat-shaped pulpit from Plersch's workshop deserves special attention. It is represented as the bow of a boat with the thick mast and spar forming the sign of the cross. The anchor hanging over the board symbolizes hope. The silver eagle with wings spread out to fly was considered a symbol of independence during the partitions.

There are several seventeenth and eighteenth century pictures in the church, i.e. one representing *St. Anne* by brother Franciszek Lekszycki and the painting of *St. Alojzy Gonzaga*, attributed to Daniel Schulz.

Recently the monument to the late Primate of Poland, Stefan the Cardinal Wyszyński, was erected in front of the church.

Tyszkiewiczes' Palace — one of the Atlantes

Monument to Prince Józef Poniatowski

◀Tyszkiewiczes' Palace

TYSZKIEWICZES' PALACE

This classicist palace planned by Stanisław Zawadzki and Jan Chrystian Kamsetzer was erected in the years 1785—1792 for the Great Marshall of Lithuania, Ludwik Tyszkiewicz. The most characteristic feature of its architecture are the figures of the four *Atlantes* carved by André Le Brun on the wall facing Krakowskie Przedmieście. They support the first floor balcony, at the same time providing the decoration for the main entrance. The figures were modelled on the *Atlantes* from the Theatre of Dionysius in Athens. The side wall facing the Visitation Nuns' church is decorated with demi-columns encompassing the *porte-fenêtres* of the first floor opening on to the balcony supported by stone consoles. The crestings of the palace are crowned with panoplies in the form of banners and arms alluding to the hetman office of the owner. The interior — the vestibule, the staircase and the ball-room on the upper level, have a magnificent, rich stucco decoration executed between 1787—1789 and designed by Jan Chrystian Kamsetzer. Reconstructed after World War II damages, the building now houses the Warsaw University Library Cabinet of Drawings.

STATUE OF DUKE JÓZEF PONIATOWSKI

Execution of the monument was entrusted to Bertel Thorvaldsen. He made the figure of *Duke Józef* similar to those of antique heroes. His timeless youth and classicist features, antique attire, the outstretched sword in his hand, as well as the serene, majestic charm of his horse, form clear associations with the figure of *Marcus Aurelius*, but they do not reflect the real, turbulent nature of the Duke nor his heroic death for the fatherland. The statue was finished in 1832, but it could not be placed in Warsaw. On the czar's commands it was sent to Modlin and then taken away by the czar's governor, Duke Ivan Paskiewicz to his residence in Homle. It was returned to Poland only after World War I, when it was placed in Saski Square, in front of the Saski Palace colonnade. Destroyed in World War II, it was again cast from the model stored in the Thorvaldsen Museum in Denmark and offered to Poland as a gift from the Danish people. At first the monument was placed in the Łazienki Park, in front of the Orangery. It was only in 1965 that the decision to put it in a more exposed place was made. Since then it has stood in Krakowskie Przedmieście.

University of Warsaw — fragment of the gate

UNIVERSITY OF WARSAW

The University of Warsaw was established in 1816 on the initiative of Stanislaus Staszic and Stanisław Kostka Potocki by merging the School of Law and Administration (founded in 1808) and the Medical School (founded in 1809). It comprised five departments : Theology, Law and Administration, Medicine, Philosophy, and Fine Arts and Sciences. In 1830 its activities were suspended by orders of czarist authorities. It was reactivated in 1862 as the Warsaw Main School, which functioned only until 1869, and then was transformed into the Russian Imperial University. It was only in 1915 that the Polish university was restored.

Between 1935—1939 it was called the Józef Piłsudski University. During the last war and occupation the university was closed by the Germans, but it functioned in the underground, so that classes and lectures were organized in conspiracy. Rebuilt after the war, it is now the largest university in Poland. University buildings are located along Krakowskie Przedmieście, reaching the Vistula scarp. The entrance to the university leads through a Neo-baroque **Gate** designed by Stefan Szyller which is surmounted in the middle by the figure of the crowned *Polish eagle* and decorated with sculptures in niches.

LIBRARY BUILDING

Built in the years 1891—1894, also according to Szyller's plans. It is decorated with a group of sculptures representing the *Apotheosis of Knowledge and Science* placed on the crestings surmounting the façade. On the back wall of the building, there is a triangular tympanum with the representation of *Juno Offering Science to the Gods in the Olympus*, and below busts of scientists are placed on decorative consoles. Inside the building there are book collections, reading rooms, a great two story catalogue hall lit through a glass roof supported by a steel construction, manuscript rooms, library rooms. All the rooms accessible to the public have rich stucco decorations.

The Casimir Palace is situated behind the building of the Library. It was erected in 1634 for King Władysław IV and then remodelled by King Jan Kazimierz in 1660. Now the Casimir Palace is the seat of the University of Warsaw Rector's Offices. University buildings include also the Uruskich Palace. This is a Neo-Renaissance building erected between 1844—1847 and designed by the architect Andrzej Gołoński. Now it houses the University of Warsaw Geography Institute. The Tyszkiewiczes' Palace, which is adjacent to this building, houses the collection of the University Library Cabinet of Drawings.

Holy Cross Church — fragment of the main altar

◄Holy Cross Church

Holy Cross Church — interior

CHURCH
OF THE HOLY CROSS

The Church is dedicated to the Finding of the Holy Cross. In its present form it was erected in the years 1679—1696 for the missionary priests brought to Poland in 1651 by Queen Louise Marie. The building was designed by an Italian architect working in Warsaw, Józef Szymon Belotti. The imposing two tower façade was erected in the years 1725—1737 according to the design by Józef Fontana and finished after the mid 18th century by Jakub Fontana (the middle part). The surface of the façade, divided by pilasters, is almost flat, with a stronger accent only on the portico at the main entrance to the church: two Ionic columns support the prominent, triangular gable broken at the bottom, on which two allegorical figures were placed — personifications of *Faith* and *Hope*. Over the side entrance figures of *St. Peter* and *St. Paul* were placed in niches. The façade has a superimposed eliptical gable, with a cross at the top. In 1858 the stairs in front of the church were decorated with the beautiful statue of *Christ Carrying the Cross*, made according to the design by Andrzej Pruszyński.

The interior of the church, with the two story, straight, closed chancel and transept has the plan of the cross; on both sides of the nave there are spacious chapels linked with each other by arcaded passages.

Of the former seven altars only three are extant in their original state: those are in the chapels on the southern side. The rest are reconstructions. The main altar, similarly to the other ones, is maintained in the style of classicising Baroque. In its middle field there is a picture of the *Crucifiction*. Most precious from the point of view of artistic and historical value is the altar in the southern arm of the transept, formerly devoted to St. Genevieve and Felicissima. It was made according to the plan by Tylman of Gameren and decorated with carved figures of saints: *Barbara*, *Catherine*, *Dorothy*, *Agnes*, placed between the columns and on the entablature, and crowned by the cross adored by two angels. Attention should also be paid to the altar of St. Michael the Archangel from the early 18th century, which is placed in the first southern chapel from the entrance. It features an original Baroque picture with the representation of *Archangel Michael*.

In the southern arm of the transept is the late Baroque tombstone of Cardinal Michał Stefan Radziejowski, made of black marble in the years 1719—1722, probably planned by the Cracow architect Kacper Bażanko.

A special feature of the Church of the Holy Cross is its group of epitaphs and tablets commemorating outstanding Poles — artists and scientists. The work which provided the start to the series was the statue unveiled in 1880 and placed over the heart of Fryderyk Chopin, which was brought to Poland after his death, as the composer had willed.

57

Staszic' Palace

STASZIC' PALACE

Krakowskie Przedmieście is closed by the monumental classicist palace built in 1820—1823 to be the seat of the Friends of Science Society. It was erected thanks to the efforts and at the expense of its co-founder, and since 1808 also President, the outstanding activist and political writer of the Enlightenment, Stanisław Staszic (hence the name of the palace). Antonio Corazzi, a Florentine architect working in Warsaw, was the author of the building. The monumental façade flanked with shallow bay projections is decorated with Corinthian pilasters, while on either side of the middle part there are two column porticoes, also in the Corinthian order. A belvedere with semi-circular windows and a small dome is superimposed on the building. In the years 1892—1893 the palace was reconstructed by the Russian architect M. Pokrowski in the Byzantine-Russian style. It then housed a Russian gymnasium and a Russian orthodox church. After World War I, in the years 1924—1926, work partly restoring the former appearance of the palace was carried out under the supervision of Marian Lalewicz. In the inter-war period it was the seat of the Science Society. In the years 1947—1959 the building was reconstructed after casualties of the last war; its original appearance was restored and it was extended in the direction of Świętokrzyska Street. Now it houses institutes and departments of the Polish Academy of Science.

MONUMENT TO NICOLAUS COPERNICUS

The idea of erecting a monument to the outstanding Polish astronomer was first brought up by Stanisław Staszic. Under the historical conditions of the times — the partitions — the monument was to express the idea of the Polish nation's ties with tradition, to teach respect for learning and science; it was to be a demonstration not only of national feelings, but also of the nation's mind. Originally the monument was to stand in the astronomer's home town — Toruń. According to the design presented by the architect Peter Aigner, it was to be an obelisk, about 16 metres in hight, made of granite. Its sides were to be covered with signs of the zodiac, and the planets of our solar system represented at the base. The change in the political situation of Poland (formation of the Congressional Kingdom, of which Toruń was not a part) made the placing of the monument in Toruń impossible. It was then decided that it would stand in Warsaw. At first the square in front of the Casimir Palace was taken into account (in the place now occupied by the University Library), but eventually the location was to be in front of the Friends of Science Society building, for the erection of which Stanisław Staszic was beginning to arrange. The original concept of the monument was changed: it was no longer to be a symbolic obelisk, but a statue representing Copernicus holding astronomical instruments. In 1820 the Danish sculptor, Bertel Thorvaldsen was asked to execute it. Thorvaldsen, for whom artistic beauty was epitomised in the art of the antiquity, in his work tried to reconcile his own ideals with the quite explicitly stated wishes of the commissioners. He represented the great scientist seated, dressed in a toga, with compasses in his right and an astrolabe in his left hand. The figure is dignified and serious; his face resembles extant portraits of Copernicus and his eyes are raised to the sky, which he researched when alive. The pedestal, made according to the design by Adam Idźkowski an Antonio Corazzi is on two sides decorated with a Latin inscription: *NICOLAO COPERNICO GRATA PATRIA* and a Polish one, which translated into English means: *TO NICOLAUS COPERNICUS FROM HIS COMPATRIOTS*. During the German occupation the monument remained on its pedestal, but the Polish inscription was covered by a tablet with an inscription in German. As part of the so-called small sabotage, scouts from Szare Szeregi (Grey Squads) took the tablet off and hid it, as a sign of the Polish society's protest. This took place almost under the eye of the Germans — practically next to their police headquarters. During the Warsaw Uprising in 1944, the monument was damaged and then knocked down. It was put back on the extant pedestal in July of 1945 and in 1949 both the pedestal and the figure underwent thorough restoration.

Monument to Mikołaj Kopernik

ST. ALEXANDER'S CHURCH

The present location of St. Alexander's Church, built in the years 1818—1825, was to be the site for the arch of triumph commemorating the 1815 entrance to Warsaw of czar Alexander I, whom the Congress of Vienna nominated the head of the newly formed Polish Kingdom. Design work was entrusted to Piotr Chrystian Aigner. The church he planned was modelled on the Pantheon in Rome; it had the form of a rotunda from the north and from the south was preceded by six-columned Corinthian porticoes. Over the rotunda quite a high lantern was built, with blind arcades broken through it; the whole was covered by a flattened dome. The architecture was characterized by extreme restraint and sparsity of decoration. Also the interior was formed to be a miniature Pantheon; eight niches were placed in the walls, of which four, situated opposite each other, were divided by two columns supporting the entablature. Busts of outstanding personalities with merits for the fatherland were to be placed in the niches. Soon the church turned out to be too small for the needs of its quite large parish, so in the years 1886—1894 it was remodelled and significantly enlarged, giving it Neo-Renaissance forms. Józef Pius Dziekoński was the author of the reconstruction. Also this church did not last long and was almost totally destroyed during the Warsaw Uprising of 1944. After the war it was reconstructed following Aigner's original plans.

Figures of Atlantes on the building
of the Medical Doctors' Association

Ostrogskis' Palace in Tamka Street

GNIŃSKIS' PALACE

The palace was erected in the years 1681—1685 according
to the plans by Tylman of Gameren for the Crown Under-
chancellor Jan Gniński, in place of the sixteenth century
Ostrogskis' castle. Unfortunately out of the great palace
and garden project only one outbuilding was erected (now
called the Ostrogskis' Palace). This is a two story building
planned on a rectangle, with a bay projection decorated
with Corinthian pilasters and a superimposed triangular
gable; it is preceded by a terrace supported by a
semi-defense platform. Since 1859 the Warsaw Musical
Conservatoire was located here, where e.g. Ignacy Paderew-
ski and Karol Symanowski were educated. Now the palace is the seat of the Fryderyk Chopin Society.

The place is connected with one of the most beautiful of
Warsaw's legends about a golden duck; in the underground vaults of the Ostrogskis' castle there used to be
a lake, in which a princess changed into a golden duck
swam. The princess could return to her human form only
if someone lifted the spell by taking 100 ducats from the
place indicated for three days in a row, and each day
spending it only on himself. A soldier undertook to fulfil
the task. On the third day, however, overwhelmed by pity,
he gave his last *grosz* to a beggar. This caused the lake
and the duck to disappear forever.

Łazienki, the Belvedere — wall facing the garden

Łazienki, Palace on Water — southern wall

On the following pages:
Łazienki, Palace on Water — northern wall

ŁAZIENKI

The Warsaw Łazienki Park extends over the former Animal Park (i.e. hunting grounds), used for that purpose already by the Mazowsze Dukes, who owned the nearby Jazdów stronghold (Ujazdów). The grounds were preserved also when the dukes' residence was transferred to Warsaw. After Mazowsze joined the Crown, Jazdów became the temporary residence for the Kings of the Republic. In 1548 Queen Bona, the wife of King Sigismundus III Vasa, became the owner of the stronghold. It then passed on to her daughter, Anna Jagiellonka. At the beginning of the 17th century, King Sigismundus III Vasa erected a new, masonry castle here, called the **Ujazdowski Castle**. In 1674 Ujazdów was bought from the current owners by Marshall Stanisław Herakliusz Lubomirski. He commissioned the building of two pavilions on the terrains of the Animal Park, according to plans by Tylman of Gameren. One was the **Ermitage** — a place for solitary meditations and the other one the **Bath**. It was from the latter pavilion, situated on an island surrounded by a canal, that the place later got its name. But Łazienki reached its splen-

dour only in the times of Stanislaus Augustus Poniatowski. In 1764, still before being elected, he bought the Ujazdowski Castle with the adjacent land, planning to erect a private summer residence there. For many years the most outstanding royal architects, painters and sculptors were engaged in the project. Dominik Merlini was its main designer. Jan Chrystian Kamsetzer cooperated with him in decorating the interiors while the painted decorations were the work of Marcello Bacciarelli and Jan Bogumił Plersch. The sculptures for the interior and for the park were made by André Le Brun, Jakub Monaldi, Franciszek Pinck and Tomasso Righi. As a result of all the artists' efforts and with the active cooperation of the King, an extensive palace and park area was established, which was the embodiment of the new concept of the suburbian residence whose characteristic features are small architecture, and the building of several independent pavilions fulfilling different — not only residential — functions, placed in the vast garden and park area.
The **Palace on Water**, based on reconstructing the former

63

Łazienki, Palace on Water — part of the gallery

Łazienki, Palace on Water
— figure of a *Gladiator* on the northern terrace

Łazienki, Palace on Water
— a figure near the wall of the palace

Lubomirski's Bath — constituted the heart of the Łazienki project. It was surrounded by two elongated ponds; the northern one was closed by a bridge with the **Monument to Jan Sobieski III**, the southern one by the **Amphitheatre**. If a line was extended along the crosswise axis of the Palace towards the west, it would reach the **Little White House**, and towards the east — the **Myślewicki Palace**. This was not a strictly geometrical plan; the park, designed by Jan Chrystian Schuch, was set up as an irregular English park mostly made up of irregular paths leading from one pavilion and small building to another.

PALACE ON WATER

The King started renovating the Baroque Bath in 1772, at first without introducing any changes. Work on the Bath building was then carried out in stages until the end of Stanislaus Augustus' reign in 1795. In 1776 decorative stairs leading to the pond were built on the nothern side; their balustrade was decorated with statues of ancient gods and satires. Next year the building was extended by

Łazienki, Palace on Water — Ball-room   Łazienki, Palace on Water — Rotunda

an extra story. In 1784 work on a new southern façade with a concave portico supported by four Corinthian columns was begun. At the sides there are one axis parts of the façade with semi-circular *porte-fenêtres* on the ground floor, and rectangular ones leading onto balconies with iron balustrades on the first floor. The façade is flanked with pilasters at the corners. The shell, which is perhaps a conscious reference to the former Bath, is a recurring motif in the decoration. The front is topped with a balustraded cresting, on which four figures symbolising the seasons by the sculptor Le Brun were placed. In 1788 a new façade was built on the northern side. It was divided by Corinthian pilasters, and in the middle part a triangular tympanum decorated with the royal cartouche was placed between female figures personifying *Fame* and *Peace*. The façade is surmounted by a balustraded cresting with sculptures representing the four continents: *Europe*, *Asia*, *America* and *Africa*. Along the whole façade there is a terrace supported on a stone socle underpinning on either side. On both sides flights of stairs lead to the lower terrace, separated from the water by only one step; the side stairs are decorated with sculptures of lions spouting water from their muzzles, while the terrace is adorned with two figures of fighting gladiators. On the roof of the palace is a belvedere with semi-rounded windows all around. Inside is the dome covering the central room of the Palace — the so-called Grotto of the former Bath. Also the belvedere is

crowned with a balustraded attic and decorated with four sculptures symbolising the elements: *Water*, *Fire*, *Air* and the *Earth*. The arrangement of the interiors was also changed. Four years later work was resumed due to the necessity of extending the Palace even further. Since there was no space on the island, two separate pavilions were erected outside of it — in the east and in the west. They were then linked with the main corpus by means of bridges supported by an arcade and columnated galeries. The galeries were glassed in and inside there were busts of Roman emperors sculptured by Righi (now they stand on the terrace in front of the Orangery).

The most presentable room is the **Ball-room** which was built during the reconstruction of 1788 according to the design by Jan Chrystian Kamsetzer. Its decoration perfectly harmonizes with the architecture. Two fireplaces with the architectural framework of wall porticoes were placed on the narrower walls. On the southern wall, in a niche over the fireplace stands an eighteenth century copy of the statue of *Herkules*; the mantelpiece is supported by the figures of *Centaurus* and *Cerberus*. The whole composition symbolizes the triumph of man over powers of the dark. The copy of the figure of *Apollo Belvedere* is placed on the opposite wall, while the mantelpiece is supported by sculptures representing *King Midas* and the satyr *Marsyas*. The group symbolizes the superiority of the spirit over Stupidity and Pride. Over the frontal of both mantel-

Łazienki, Palace on Water
— wall painting by J.B. Plersch in the Ball-room:
Atropos Cutting the Thread of Human Life

Łazienki, Palace on Water
— stucco decoration in the Bathroom

Łazienki, Palace on Water — Solomon's Room

Łazienki, Palace on Water
— fireplace with statue of *Hercules* in the Ball-room

pieces there are sculptures of eagles taking off to fly. On the crosswise axis of the Ball-room there are: a gallery for the orchestra and the exit onto the gallery. The wall over the gallery is decorated with bas-reliefs representing *Hercules and Deianira* and *Apollo and Daphne*; there is a clock with Cronus' head between them and on the opposite side is the coat of arms of the Republic. The walls are decorated with symmetrically placed vertical panneaux with grotesque decorations by Jan Bogumił Plersch; the four middle ones symbolize the elements, while the four outer ones refer to the concept of time and human age.

The Rotunda constituting the central room of the Palace is a kind of Pantheon devoted to monarchs whose reign made Poland prosper and flourish. Merlini was the main designer of the interior, while the concept for it probably came from Stanislaus Augustus. The walls were lined with grey and yellow stucco and divided by white stucco columns. In the niches between the columns there are figures

Łazienki, Little White House

Łazienki, Little White House — Dining-room

of four Polish Kings particularly respected by Stanislaus Augustus: *Casimir the Great, Sigismundus the Old, Stefan Batory* and *Jan Sobieski III.* Over the door leading to neighbouring rooms there are busts of three Roman emperors: *Trajan, Titus* and *Marcus Aurelius.* It is to them that the inscription in the frieze around the room refers: "Seat as examples to benefit the world". The figures and busts were executed by Jakub Monaldi, André Le Brun and Franciszek Pinck. The dome is decorated with four tondi painted by Marcello Bacciarelli representing the personifications of virtues: *Courage* represented as Mars (with the facial features of Stanislaus Augustus), *Justice* represented as Themis, *Wisdom* represented as Minerva and *Goodness* as Clementia. The decoration of the Room is completed by the floor in many-coloured marble forming a star pattern. In the very middle there was the painted head of Maedusa which was later destroyed.

The decoration of the rotunda was finished when the King no longer stayed in Warsaw, so he never saw it in its final form. The interior, as the only one in the Palace, was not consumed by fire in 1944, but it was also badly damaged. Some of the original furnishings were lost.

Solomon's Room fulfilled the role of the sitting room in the Palace. It was decorated with paintings by Bacciarelli telling the story of the Biblical king famous for his wisdom and just sentences. The pictures placed here represented *Solomon's Sacrifice* and the *Consecration of the Temple in Jerusalem.* On the ceiling is *Solomon Dreaming about Greatness* surrounded by allegories of *Fame, Fortune* and *Wisdom.* The facets represent *Solomonic Decision,* the *Queen of Sheba with Solomon* and *Solomon with King Hiram.* The representations were a kind of panegyric in honour of Stanislaus Augustus, whose facial features were given to the Biblical monarch. In the supraportas over the door, Jan Bogumił Plersch painted: a dolphin — symbolising wisdom, a peacock standing for immortality, a salamander — representing indestructibility and a lion — symbolising strength. Plersch is also the author of arabesques decorating the door panels. The present decoration of the Room — with the exception of the marble fireplaces with relief representations of *Pallas* and the *Sleeping Achilles* — is a reconstruction.

WHITE HOUSE

Towards the west of the palace is the White House built in the years 1774—1777 according to the design by Dominik Merlini. It was the first new building erected for Stanislaus Augustus in the park. Set up on the plan of a square, it is a one story building crowned with a wooden balustrade and a belvedere on top of the roof. All the walls were identically treated: decorated with rustication, they had five-axes, rectangular *porte-fenêtres* on the ground floor andsmall, arched windows on the first floor. This small, light building was fortunately preserved intact until today. The figure of a satyr carrying the face of a sundial is represented in front of the southern wall.

A considerable number of rooms in the White House has maintained their original furnishings. One of the most beautiful and most interesting interiors is the dining room situated left of the vestibule on the ground floor. The walls were decorated by Jan Bogumił Plersch with paintings of a grotesque type on a goldish background. This type of paintings, referring — by means of the decorations of Raphael's Loggias in the Vatican — to paintings of the antiquity, underwent a Renaissance in the 18th century Neoclassical period; the paintings in the Dining Room of the White House are some of the earliest examples of this type of decorations in Poland. The motif of the grotesque was intertwined with semi-circles filled with landscape paintings, which can be seen over the mirrors. There are also small rectangles with sings of the zodiac and medallions with representations of peasants at work. The groups of paintings placed on each of the longer walls of the room symbolize the four elements: *Water*, *Air*, *Fire* and the *Earth*, while the paintings on the shorter walls represent *Night* and *Day*. The four representations of animals in the corners of the room: the elephant, camel, horse and ostrich refer to four continents — *Africa*, *Asia*, *Europe* and *America*. The paintings are exceptional for their richness and inventiveness of detail and their small form and delicacy of colour is very well suited for the architecture of the interior. The beautiful, patterned floor with geometrical and flower motifs made of different-coloured wood, is an additional decorative element. There is a niche in front of the middle window, where the antique sculpture of *Venus Anadyomene* (rising from the sea) was placed. It was bought for the King in Rome in 1777. The head of the figure was reconstructed by André Le Brun. The writing table made of rose wood was also part of the original furniture. This is a domestic product, probably made by royal carpenters in the 1780's.

Łazienki, Palace on Water

Łazienki, Amphitheatre

BELVEDERE

Towards the south-west of the Palace on Water, now already outside the Łazienki Park area, is the old summer residence of the Pac family — the Belvedere. A *belvedere* or gazebo is a palace, villa or garden pavilion with a beautiful, extensive view. The Warsaw Belvedere is picturesquely situated on the edge of a high Vistula scarp. It was erected in 1659 for the Great Chancellor of Lithuania, Krzysztof Pac. In 1767 the palace was bought from its current owners by Stanislaus Augustus Poniatowski, who made it part of the Łazienki area. Later he established the Royal Manufactory of Faience in one of its outbuildings. After the King's death, it was inherited by his nephew, Prince Józef Poniatowski. In 1818 the current owners sold the palace. It was bought by the government of the Congressional Kingdom and became the residence of the czar's brother, the Great Duke Konstanty. Work on modernization and reconstruction of the building started almost immediately. As a result, the palace gained a new look, consistent with the spirit of classicism. One of its main designers was an outstanding student of Merlini's, Jakub Kubicki.

The Belvedere made its most important mark in history during the events on the night of November 29, 1930 when a group of insurgents arrived here to kill the despised Duke Konstanty, who nevertheless managed to save himself. The palace has remained unchanged until today. Since 1918 it has been the official state seat. Now it is the seat of the President of the Republic of Poland.

AMPHITHEATRE

The summer theatre, modelled on theatres of the antiquity (the theatre in Herkulanum), with an amphitheatre auditorium built on a semi-circle and a stage on an island, was situated south of the Palace on Water. It was built in the years 1790—1793, probably designed by Jan Chrystian Kamsetzer. The amphitheatre consists of two parts: the ground level is flanked with sculptures representing the *Dying Gladiator* and the *Dying Cleopatra* (they used to decorate the terrace in front of the Palace). In the middle, between iron barriers is the Kings's box; the stairs behind the box go up, towards the auditorium. The attic of the Amphitheatre is decorated with sixteen seated figures facing the audience. They represent famous poets of the antiquity: *Aeshylos, Euripides, Sophocles, Aristophanes, Meander, Plautus, Terence* and *Seneca*; and of modern times: *Shakespeare, Caldoron, Racine, Moliere, Metastas* and *Lessing* as well as two contemporary Polish writers, participants of the famous Thursday dinners organized by the King — *Adam Naruszewicz* and *Stanisław Trembecki*. The sculptures were designed by André Le Brun and carved by Tomasz Righi.

The stage, which is separated from the auditorium by water, was equipped with permanent decoration imitating the ruins of an ancient temple; the pattern for these ruins was found in the Baalbek temple in Syria, which is renowned for its sculptures. The orchestra pit was built in front of the stage.

Łazienki, Myślewicki Palace
— entrance niche

Łazienki, Myślewicki Palace
— façade

MYŚLEWICKI PALACE

It is situated in the eastern area of the park, in a rather secluded spot. Built in stages in the years 1775—1784 according to the design by Dominik Merlini, it consists of a not very large, three-story corpus built on the plan of a square and side pavilions added a little later, joined with the middle part by means of quartercircular wings. The wings, which were at first one-story high, with view terraces surrounded by a balustrade on the roofs, were later extended by the second floor; in this way side pavilions were "absorbed" by the wings, becoming as if their integral part, and the whole façade gained monumentality. Adding the wings to the middle corpus changed the character of the building; no longer a villa, it became a small palace shaped according to the traditional Baroque design, with the higher middle part flanked with two lower ones, thus gaining picturesqueness. Decorations of the front of the palace are of very high artistic quality. It is moreover the only building in Warsaw, which has maintained its original decorations in such a perfect state.

The façade has an impressive monumental, three-story niche whose coffered vault is decorated with rosettes. The niche, which is a darker spot on the light surface of the wall, enhances the picturesqueness of the building. Above, there is a horizontal, oval window surrounded by a protuberant stylized shell frame. The niche has pilasters on the sides with panels full of decorative elements. Inside, on both sides of the door, in the conch vaulted niches, there are figures of *Flora* and *Zephyrus*. The rectangular *porte-fenêtre* placed over the door is surmounted by a round medallion with the letters "JP", allowing to suppose that the palace was designed to be the house of Stanislaus Augustus' nephew, Duke Józef Poniatowski. Fan stairs, limited below by an iron balustrade with two pedestals, lead to the niche on which there are sculptures

Łazienki, Myślewicki Palace
— Dining-room

Łazienki, Myślewicki Palace
— room with landscape paintings

representing two children holding lanterns. Side parts of the façade have no richer decoration — except for the prominent window frames. The interiors of the palace have to a large extent maintained their original decoration. One of the more beautiful and presentable rooms is the Dining Room situated on the ground floor in the eastern corner of the main corpus (later transformed into a bedroom). The lengthwise axis is accentuated by a fireplace made of marble with a mirror placed over it. The walls are covered with paintings representing sights of Rome and Venice. On the main wall is the painting of the *View of St. Michael's Bridge in Rome*, while opposite, between windows — *Pius VI Casino in the Vatican*, and on both sides of the Eastern window — *Views of St. Mark's Square in Venice*. The paintings, made in 1778, were made on the basis of the publications of engravings by Jan Bogumił Plersch, author of the grotesque paintings in the Dining

Room of the White House, which were very popular at that time. The two so very different types of decoration, which originated roughly at the same time and were painted by the same artist, give evidence to his outstanding talent.

There is one more room on the ground floor of the palace which has walls decorated with landscape elements; this is a small room in the western apartment adorned with seven fantastic views of ancient ruins represented against the background of a Romantic landscape.

In the vicinity of the Myślewicki palace is the so-called Wielka Oficyna (Great Outhouse), which in the times of Stanislaus Augustus provided housing for servants and a kitchen. Later the building was transformed into the School of Officer Cadets; on the eve of November 29, 1830 the first squad of the November Uprising started out from here.

Łazienki — Temple of Sybille (Diana)

Łazienki, blooming water lilies on the pond

TEMPLE OF SYBILLE

This small temple is situated in a remote area of the park, below the Belvedere. After 1817, when the Łazienki became the property of czar Aleksander I, this part of the park was separated from the rest and incorporated into the Belvedere Palace, then the residence of the czar's brother, the Great Duke Konstanty. The Belvedere garden was designed in the Romantic spirit, with wide meadows, divided by groups of trees and bushes. Opposite the palace a pond with irregular borders was formed; in its eastern part an island overgrown with trees was situated, with a bridge leading onto it. Over the pond, on a hill on the northern side, the so-called Temple of Sybille was built. This is a wooden building constructed on the plan of a rectangle and surrounded by an Ionic colonnade, whose architecture is reminiscent of that of classical ancient Greece. At the entrance to the temple there are two cast iron lions. In the interior there is a room lit by rectangular windows placed in its side wall. They are decorated with paintings of flowers and fruit. The date of erecting this building may be established to have been approximately 1820—1822. Besides the Temple of Sybille, two more pavilions were built in the Belvedere garden: the Neogothic Orangery and the so-called Egyptian Temple and the Egyptian Bridge.

Łazienki, monument to Jan III Sobieski in Agrykola

STATUE
OF JAN SOBIESKI III

One of the most important components of the Łazienki Park is the statue of *King Jan Sobieski III*, placed on the bridge in Agrykola closing the perspective of the pond from the North. It was made by Franciszek Pinck, while the design was probably André Le Brun's. The statue represents the figure of a rider in knightly armour; under the hoofs of his rampant horse lies a Turk, while at the sides are the arms plundered from the Turks. The Baroque, stucco statue of *Jan III* in the Wilanów palace served as the pattern here. The small bridge in Agrykola was enlarged especially for the purpose of placing the monument on it; it was extended by two bays towards the East, while the middle part on the Northern side had the arcaded part added. It was over this part that the pedestal

with the monument was built. The bridge was all along surrounded with stone pillars and an iron railing. The unveiling of the monument, which is the largest statue in the Łazienki Park, was very solemnly celebrated on 14 September 1788, the anniversary of lifting the siege of Vienna. The figure of *Jan III*, very often occurring in designs of art works founded by Stanislaus Augustus, was that of Stanislaus Augustus' favourite and most esteemed monarch in Polish history. The unveiling of the monument in the Łazienki and the celebrations connected with it had, in this particular case, also another aim besides the wish to pay tribute to the heroic King, connected with the political aspirations of Stanislaus Augustus. Resuscitating the memory of the Vienna victory, he wanted to arouse anti-Turkish sentiments in order to have Poland join the coalition between Russia and Austria against the Ottoman Empire. The political aim was not achieved, but the Łazienki gained a new monument.

MONUMENT TO CHOPIN

The history of this monument is very turbulent and complicated. The idea of commemorating the great Polish composer by erecting a monument to him in the capital was first introduced by the Warsaw Music Society in 1876. Due to difficulties on the part of the partitioning authorities only a tablet could be built into the pillar of the church of St. Cross where Chopin's heart was kept. The idea of building a monument to Chopin was again taken up in 1899, on the 50th anniversary of the composer's death. In 1902 the Social Committee for the Erection of a Monument to Fryderyk Chopin was set up in Warsaw. The sculptural competition for the design of the monument was publically announced in 1908. As a result, the work by the renowned painter and sculptor, Wacław Szymanowski was chosen. The monument he designed bears all the marks of Art Nouveau. Placing the monument over the pond in which its reflection is even more fluid and full of movement, adds to the impressionism of the figure. Chopin sitting under the willow is inadvertedly associated with the melancholy Polish landscape — "he listens to voices of nature", and the music is born only from this listening. In this way the artist conveyed the essence of Chopin's music, the inspiration for which was the landscape of the homeland. A great discussion concerning the monument was started in the press, the artist was in turns either praised or ruthlessly criticised. Work on implementing the project, whose plaster of paris model was to be moulded in France, progressed rather slowly, due to financial difficulties. Finally it was interrupted by the outbreak of World War I. After the war the issue of implementing the project came to a standstill. It was only thanks to the extraordinary energy and strong will of the artist, who aimed to finish one of his greatest works, that the monument was finally erected. The ceremony of its unveiling took place on the 14 of November 1926, fifty years after the idea of building it was bcrn, and almost a quarter of a century after initiating the efforts aiming to implement it. The monument remained in its place for only 18 years, because after the outbreak of World War II Chopin's music became illegal, and pictures and sculptures of the artist were destroyed by the Germans. Such was also the fate of the monument in the Łazienki, which was the first Warsaw monument to be torn down. After the war the sculpture was meticulously reconstructed and erected in its former place.

Łazienki, monument to Fryderyk Chopin

Technical University Building — façade

Technical University Building — staircase

Technical University Building — courtyard

CITY CENTRE

WARSAW TECHNICAL UNIVERSITY

Traditions of the Warsaw Technical University go back to the year 1825, when on Stanislaus Augustus initiative the Polytechnical School was established in Warsaw. Closed in 1831, after the November Uprising, it was reopened in 1897. In the years 1899—1991 the seat of the school was built from public contribution. The main building, which was erected in the years 1899—1900 according to Stefan Szyller's design comprises part of a larger undertaking; Szyller incorporated the building of the Department of Physics into it, while the rest of the buildings (housing the Mechanics and Chemistry Departments) are the work of Bronisław Brochowicz Rogoyski. The main building of the Technical University is eclectic in form, with Renaissance and Classicist elements. It was built on the plan of a pentagon with three internal wings setting out: the cloistered main court covered by a glass roof situated on the

Technical University Building — group of sculptures in the cresting

Houses in Aleje Jerozolimskie

axis of the front wing, as well as side courts. On the super-imposed cresting there is a group of sculptures by Pius Weloński representing the *Apotheosis of Science*. The main court is surrounded by cloisters with arcades supported by pillars, and — on the highest storey — rectangular windows. In the bay projection of one of the court walls is a multilevel open staircase with a semi-circular balcony on the axis.

ALEJE JEROZOLIMSKIE

The buildings in Aleje Jerozolimskie (Jerozolimskie Avenue) between Marszałkowska and Emilii Plater Streets can serve as an example of early 19th century Warsaw architecture, when no single specific style persisted, and architects either created buildings devoid of a specific style or applied it only to a certain extent (Art Nouveau). The "Polonia" Hotel erected in the years 1909—1913 according to the designs by Nagórski and Józef Holewiński is an early Art Nouveau building with references to classical forms. Neighbouring buildings erected in the years

1900—1910 are also usually maintained in early Art Nouveau forms with Baroque and classical elements. Most interesting and original is the building at the crossing of Aleje Jerozolimskie and Poznańska Street built in the years 1905—1906 according to the design by Ludwik Panczakiewicz, which has Art Nouveau decoration. Art Nouveau, which was introduced in Warsaw at the beginning of the 20th century, was a reaction to historicism and eclecticism of the form used in the fine arts and in architecture. It is characterized by asymmetry, using a soft, flowing line and plant motifs. All these features can be found in the decoration of the building in question: the asymmetrically placed dome, the unsual shape of the window — in the form of a horseshoe smaller towards the bottom — the bay projection on the axis of the façade and the curved line of the internal divisions of this windows, finally the decoration of the front wall with motifs of stylized plants with masks in between. Some other Art Nouveau buildings in Warsaw are, e.g. the Market Hall in Koszykowa Street built in 1908 and the Landau Bank in Senatorska Street erected in the years 1904—1906, with extant interiors from this period.

On this and the following page:
Palace of Culture and Science

On the following pages:
View of the city centre

MARCHING SQUARE

Along the western side of Marszałkowska Street, between Świętokrzyska and Aleje Jerozolimskie, the so-called Marching Square was built. It was made after the rest of the streets formerly crossing Marszałkowska Street and destroyed in 1944 were demolished. The square is dominated by the monumental Palace of Culture and Science erected in the years 1952–1955 according to the plan by the Soviet architect Lev Rudniev and presented as a gift of the Soviet Union for Warsaw. The height of the palace with the spire is 134 m. In front of the main entrance to the building (from Marszałkowska Street) are sculptures representing *Adam Mickiewicz* (by Stanisław Horno-Popławski) and *Mikołaj Kopernik* (by Ludwika Nitschowa). The palace houses among other things: the Polish Academy of Science, the Polish UNESCO Committee, the Polish Pen-Club Section; there are also theatres (Dramatyczny, Studio, Lalka), museums: the Museum of Technology, and the Zoological Museum run by the Polish Academy of Science, as well as exhibition halls, restaurants, cafés, sports halls, a swimming pool. The amphitheatre Congress Hall is a place for official celebrations and entertainment shows. On the 30th floor of the Palace is a view gallery, from which the panorama of Warsaw can be seen; an area of a radius of about 30 km can be seen from there. On the Eastern side of Marszałkowska Street, along Marching Square, the so-called "Eastern Wall' was built in the years 1962–1969. This is a group of buildings comprising four department stores, a PKO rotunda, three 24-storey skyscrapers, shops, cafés, cinemas and theatres. At the back of the department stores there is a promenade, which is isolated from city centre car traffic; its attractiveness is enhanced by arcades, the greenery of flower beds, the cosy interiors and terraces of cafés.

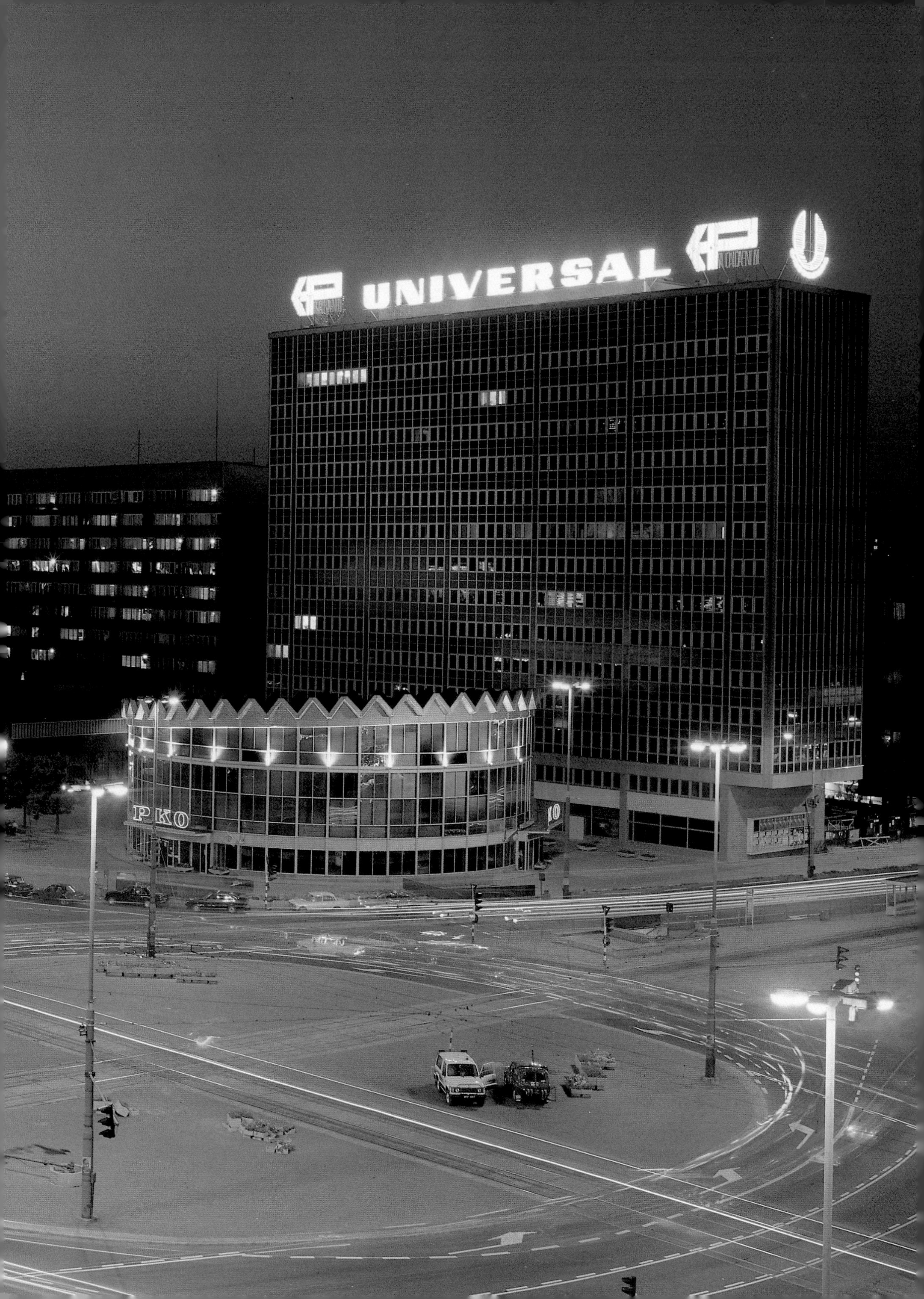
UNIVERSAL
PKO

Grand Theatre

Krasińskis' Palace — tympanum of the wall facing the garden

GRAND THEATRE

The Grand Theatre was erected in the years 1825—1832 according to the design by Antoni Corazzi. It was built in place of Marywil — a commercial centre erected on the initiative of Queen Maria Kazimiera and planned by Tylman of Gameren — which had been torn down in 1825. The only part that remained of Marywil is the outbuilding — the so-called Columned House (Market House), which was added to it in 1810 by Piotr Aigner. The outbuilding was adapted by Corazzi as the left wing of the theatre, adding to it the main corpus and — on the opposite side — the second wing, repeating the Aigner façade. Columns: i.e. the large Corinthian porticoes of the corpus with the superimposed triangular gable and Doric colonnades supporting terraces in the side wings, are the dominating motif of the front wall of the Grand Theatre. The tympanum is decorated with the relief by the Italian sculptor Thomas Acciardi, representing the Greek poet Anacreon surrounded by dancing figures. In 1890 a porticoed passage was added to the main corpus; it is decorated with a frieze representing the *Return of Aedypus from the Olympic Games* — a work by Paweł Maliński. During the war the theatre was seriously damaged and burned out inside. Only the classicist façade remained. The present building, planned by Bohdan Pniewski, was added to it in the years 1951—1965. In front of the theatre are the monuments to Stanisław Moniuszko and Wojciech Bogusławski.

On the following pages:
Krasińskis' Palace — the wall facing the garden

KRASIŃSKIS' PALACE

The palace is one of the most outstanding works of the architect of Dutch descent active in Poland, Tylman of Gameren. It was erected in the years 1677—1682 for the Warsaw starost (elder) Jan Dobrogost Krasiński.

The programme of decorations of both the tympanums crowning the middle bay projections is of extraordinary interest. It is devoted to the Krasiński family; namely to the legendary ancestor of the Krasińskis, the Roman patrician Marcus Valerius called Corvinus, i.e. Raven (the raven was in the Krasiński's coat of arms). The tympanum on the main wall represents the scene of his duel with the leader of the Gauls, when a raven comes to the Roman's aid. The victor is accompanied by figures representing *Pallas Athena* and *Mars*; in the garden tympanum there is the scene of *Marcus Valerius' triumph*. The compositions were formally based on ancient models. Andrzej Schluter was the author of these sculptures and they were made in the years 1689—1694. The genealogical motif was also continued inside. The palace remained the property of the Krasiński family until 1765. Later it was bought from the founder's family and became the seat of the Crown Treasury Committee. Now it houses the Department of Manuscript and Old Prints of the National Library.

93

Palace of the Cracow Bishops

The Primate's Palace

PALACE OF CRACOW BISHOPS

It was erected in the 17th century for bishop Jakub Zadzik. In the years 1760—1762 it was thoroughly transformed into late Baroque forms, according to the design by Jakub Fontana, and in the second half of the 19th century rebuilt into an apartment building. In the course of post-war reconstruction its late Baroque forms were restored, with the characteristic high, hipped roof with lucarnes. The walls of the presentable first floor have been divided by pilasters and decorated with garlands. The central part of the main wall — facing Miodowa Street — is crowned with a full cresting with a coat of arms cartouche supported by two *putti*.

PRIMATE'S PALACE

The first, late Renaissance Primate's palace was erected in Warsaw towards the end of the 16th century. At the end of the 17th century primate Michał Radziejowski commissioned the reconstruction of the palace by the most outstanding architect of those times — Tylman of Gameren. He extended the building by corner alcoves added to the front and garden walls. The subsequent reconstruction took place in the first half of the 18th century. But the next, classicist extension of the primate residence, which took place in the years 1777—1783, was of the greatest importance in its history. It was the work of the architect Efraim Szreger. Maintaining as the main corpus Tylman of Gameren's palace with corner alcoves, Szreger built two three-story pavilions on the plan of a square, which he connected with the corpus by means of quartercircular galleries flanking the courtyard. This type of quartercircular lining galleries popular in the second half of the 18th century in some European countries (e.g. in England, Poland, Russia) originate from villa designs by the Italian Renaissance architect, Andrea Palladio. Thanks to these galleries, the Warsaw primate's residence was transferred into a truly monumental palace. The dominating accents of this architecture are: the large, protruding bay projection of the main corpus with the huge four column Ionic portico and a triangular gable, side bay projections flanked with Ionic pilasters and four column Tuscan porticoes decorating the walls of pavilions facing the courtyard. On both sides of the main tympanum there are relief figures of winged flying glories with wreaths in their hands; the motif of such flying figures will be popular until the late classicism of the Congressional Kingdom. The side bay projections are decorated with garlands stretched out from the lion's muzzle and the motif of fasces. Work on the palace under the supervision of Szymon Bogumił Zug continued until 1789. In the first half of the 19th century it was extended by another storey. Burned down in 1939, it was reconstructed in the years 1949—1952 and its end of 18th century form was restored.

97

Loupia Palace

Building of the Society
for the Promotion of Fine Arts (Zachęta)

BUILDING OF ZACHĘTA

The Society for the Promotion of Fine Arts (Zachęta) was active in Warsaw in the years 1860—1939. The organization, attracting artists and art lovers, had as its objective the popularising of Polish art and helping artists — especially those starting their career — by organising individual and collective exhibitions, contests, publications, and by founding scholarships. In 1900 the building designed by Stefan Szyller was erected for the society's needs. Of the former, four-wing edifice which was to have a closed courtyard glassed over at the top to be used as the exhibition hall, only the front wing was initially built. Its architecture is dominated by Renaissance and classicist elements. The central part of the façade is accentuated by a bay projection composed as a concave portico; it is flanked with wide Corinthian pilasters, while the two Corinthian columns placed between them support the entablature and the triangular tympanum with sculptural decoration. In the corners of the façade there are wide Corinthian pilasters similar to those in the bay projection. The windows of the second story are divided by Ionic columns. The façade is crowned with a low cresting. In the years 1901—1903 the building was extended by a side wing, built on its southern side. Recently, in the 1980's, work on further extension was undertaken, for which designs were made by Czesław Bielecki. The northern and western wings that are being erected are similar in style and decoration to the existing Szyller wings. In this way, the idea of the original design will have been implemented after the work is finished. Now the "Zachęta" building is the seat of the Central Bureau for Art Exhibitions, which organises temporary exhibitions of Polish and foreign art and — faithful to the tradition of the former Society — is devoted to the popularization of art, organization of lectures, art lotteries, etc.

Palace of the Revenues and Treasury Commission
in Bank Square

Palace of the Revenues and Treasury Commission
in Bank Square — Ionic portico

Palace of the Revenues and Treasury Commission in
Bank Square — Ionic collonnade facing Bank Square
with a view of a modern office building

PALACE OF THE REVENUES AND TREASURY COMMIS- SION

The Palace of the Revenues and Treasury Commission is
one of the group of treasury building erected in the years
1824—1830 by Antonio Corazzi. The group, which also comprises the building of the Minister for the Treasury and
the building housing the stock exchange and the Discount
Bank, forms an unusually harmonious whole and undoubt-
edly is one of one of Corazzi's best works. The Palace of
the Revenues and Treasury Commission is its most imposing building. It was reconstructed in the years
1824—1825 out of the 17th century Leszczyńskis' palace.
The main corpus situated at the back of the courtyard is
decorated with a huge six column Corinthian portico with
a triangular tympanum. The sculptures in the tympanum
by Paweł Maliński represent allegories of *Wisdom, Indust-
ry* and *Commerce* — portrayed as Minerva, Mercury and

Jason, as well as allegories of the *Vistula* and *Bug Rivers*.
The wings of the palace which are built at right angles to
its corpus have four Ionic columns facing the courtyard,
while those parts which face Bank Square (Plac Bankowy)
have a monumental Ionic colonnade. The Palace of the
Minister for the Treasury, which is situated next to this
building, was restructured in the years 1825—1830 out of
the 18th century palace formerly belonging to the Ogiński
family. Its highly differentiated corpus and great open terraces are reminiscent of the monumentalised Renaissance
Italian villa. Standing at the corner of the Bank Square
and Elektoralna Street, the building of the former stock
exchange and Discount Bank, erected in the years
1825—1828, was adapted in shape to the triangular site. It
is the most austere and simple of the group, devoid of
column or portico decoration. Its most striking element is
the corner dome on the drum of the former stock exchange
hall. The Polish architect Jan Jakub Gay cooperated with
Corazzi in erecting this building. Now it houses the John
Paul II Museum exhibiting Mr and Mrs Porczyńskis' art
collection.

Wilanów — entrance gate

Wilanów, palace, western wall

WILANÓW

The Royal Route running from the Royal Castle through Krakowskie Przedmieście, Nowy Świat, Aleje Ujazdowskie leads to King Jan III Sobieski's suburbian residence of Wilanów (Villa Nova). The land and property in Wilanów (formerly called Milanów) were bought by the king in 1677. Work on building the residence was started in the same year.

It was called *Villa Nova* in Latin and later changed into the more Polish sounding Wilanów. The design was made by the Polonised Italian royal architect, Augustyn Locci, with the King actively participating. Locci also supervised the way work was carried out. The first building was a gentry manor house with four corner alcoves, which was typical for this period. Later, in the years 1681—1682, it was extended by half a story and garden galleries with towers and superimposed balustraded cresting, over which stone sculptures of the Muses were placed; the façade of the corpus and front walls of the galleries gained a rich architectural and sculptural decoration. The sub-

sequent stage of extending the palace fell on the years 1684—1696; the high second story was then extended over the main corpus, while the front walls of the alcoves were crowned by crestings, and towers were covered with copper helmets with the figure of *Atlas Supporting the Globe*; the façade was decorated with relief military scenes and figures of ancient gods carved by Stefan Szwaner. As a result of this work, the residence lost its former character of a modest gentry manor and acquired the form of a Baroque Italian villa.

The palace was preceded by a two-part court comprising a housekeeping part (avantcour) and grand court (cour d'honneur) separated from each other by a decorative fence with a gate. At the back, a two level French-German garden with hedges, fountains and caves was set up. In this way a characteristically Baroque palace and garden group of *entre cour et jardin* was laid out.

The palace was more, however, than just a royal residence; it was also to glorify Jan III as the warrior King.

All of the architectural and sculptural decoration of the palace referred to the figure of the King; there was a thoroughly planned and consistently implemented ideological and artistic programme to glorify the person of Jan III and his military triumphs — where the King's virtues as ruler and warrior were portrayed by using ancient symbols (the arch of triumph motif, figures of ancient gods). Roman antiquity was also clearly referred to by placing the motto: *QUOD VETUS URBS COLUIT, NUNC NOVA VILLA TENET* (What the old city [Rome] glorified now the new villa possesses).

Entrance to the residence led through a monumental stone gate richly decorated and crowned with stone figures representing *War* (Mars) and *Peace* (Pax). Mars personified the victorious King, while Pax personified peace and prosperity which were the result of the successful wars he waged; these triumphant military symbols were further emphasised by the war trophies decorating the pillars and buttresses of the gate. The victorious battles waged by the King were also referred to by relief scenes decorating the façade of the palace. The episodes from the battle of Parkany and the battle of Vienna illustrated there, as well as scenes of the victorious parade of Jan III in the streets of Vienna, consciously referred to the reliefs decorating Roman arches of triumph (those of Tytus, Trajan, Constantine), placed in niches on the cresting. The figures of an-

Wilanów, palace, portal of the southern gallery
with a relief depiction of Jan III's triumph

Wilanów, palace, main corpus

Wilanów, palace, cresting of the front wall
with the representation
of *Jan III's Triumphal Parade in the Streets of Vienna*

Wilanów, palace, figure of the *Atlas*
in the portal of the southern tower

On the following pages:
Wilanów, palace,
general view from the courtyard

cient gods personified Jan III's virtues as a monarch and
warrior: his power, justice, valour. The decoration of the
northern gallery was devoted to the King's spouse, Queen
Maria Kazimiera; her virtues as a woman and a ruler:
beauty, fertility, faithfulness were personified by the figures of *Venus, Juno,* and *Ceres* and a medallion representing *Dido.*
An additional element glorifying the owners of the palace
was the use of the arch of triumph motif in both galleries,
which was an expression of the esteem and adoration due
to rulers and victorious leaders. Also the figures of *Atlas
Supporting the Globe* — a personification of power, physical and spiritual strength — served as an apotheosis of the
King. Atlas preventing the globe from falling symbolized
Jan III preventing the fatherland from decline.
The culmination of this artistic and ideological programme glorified the Polish monarch and his whole family,
was the decoration of the main entrance to the residence,

Wilanów, palace, northern wing,
wall facing the courtyard

where the sun, as the symbol of supreme power and valour casts its rays on the shield supported by *putti* with
the coat of arms of the Sobieskis — Janina; the Latin
inscription proclaims; *REFULSIT SOL IN CLIPEIS*
(The sun shone on the shields). The application of the
Corinthian order, in the antiquity due to the Roman emperors, puts Jan III on the same level with them, as the
inheritor and continuator of their deeds and virtues. Also
the decorations of the wall facing the garden were devoted
to the royal couple, whose medallion portraits were placed in the highest part of the main corpus, while medallions with representations of rulers, heroes and busts of
Roman emperors — the monarch's predecessors to whose
deeds and fame the King aspired to refer — were placed
below. Alcove walls were decorated with coats of arms of
the Polish Kingdom (the Eagle) and the Duchy of Lithuania (Pogoń), which were both ruled by Jan III. In the
niches of the Northern gallery there were allegorical figures symbolising the earth and the provinces united under
the royal sceptre. Frescoes on the walls of galleries
illustrated selected scenes from Homer's *Odyssey* and
Virgil's *Aeneid*.
Also decorations of side walls of the alcoves come from
Jan III's times: the representation of *Uranos* with the earth-

ly and heavenly spheres (from the north) and the sundial
with the statue of *Cronos* (from the south). After Jan III's
death in 1696, Wilanów was inherited by his sons Aleksander and Konstanty. The latter sold the residence in 1720
to a friend of the Sobieskis, Elżbieta Sieniawska, wife of
the great crown hetman, who soon started to extend the
palace. In the years 1723 — 1729 side wings were erected
on both sides of the courtyard according to plans by Giovanni Spazzio; their architecture and decoration referred
to the earlier building, uniting with it in a harmonious
way and giving it the character of an elegant palace of the
period of Louis XIV. Construction work was supervised
by Józef Fontana. The new walls of the palace were divided with demi-columns and decorated with busts of Roman emperors, stuccos representing battle scenes and
scenes from Ovid's *Metamorphoses* and allegorical figures
placed in niches, representing virtues of the present
owners of the palace. The creators of these decorations,
the form and programme of which was adapted to the one
existing before, were Francesco Fumo and Pietro Innoce-
nte Comparetti, as well as Jan Jerzy Plersch.
After the death of Elżbieta Sieniawska in 1729, Wilanów
was inherited by her daughter Maria Zofia Denhoffowa
(later the wife of Duke August Czartoryski), who continu-

ing her mother's work extended the southern wing according to designs by the Saxon architect Jan Zygmunt Deybel, after the death of Spazzio in 1726 serving the role of the royal architect in Wilanów. The wall facing the garden has typical features of Saxon architecture of the first half of the 18th century; it is flat, divided by lesenes with a shallow bay projection, with composite pilasters in the middle, crowned with a plate and open work cresting.

In 1730, as a result of persistent efforts on the part of August II the Powerful, Zofia Denhoffowa endowed him with the residence for life. August, who had long been interested in acquiring Wilanów, had his architects prepare plans for rebuilding the palace ahead of time. Fortunately, the plans, which would drastically change the appearance and character of the residence, had no chances of being implemented, as the King was given Wilanów under the condition he would give up any work changing its external or internal structure. After August's death, Wilanów returned to its former owners — Maria Zofia and August Czartoryski, and then became the property of their daughter Izabela, wife of the Great Crown Marshall Stanisław Lubomirski. On the initiative of Duchess Izabella, in the years 1781—1794 reconstruction and decoration work was carried out in the palace under the supervision of the renowned Warsaw architect Szymon Bogumił Zug. The classicist bathroom building was erected near the southern wing, and in the southern part of the courtyard the kitchen outhouse and guardhouse were erected. The work also included interiors of the southern wing housing apartments of the Duchess and the interiors of several rooms of the main corpus (e.g. the Great Vestibule). To the south of the palace the Romantic English park was laid out, which enlarged the Baroque garden of Jan III's times.

Work on extension and conservation of the palace was interrupted by the outbreak of the Kościuszko Insurrection in 1794; a new stage in the history of the residence began in 1799, when Aleksandra née Lubomirska and Stanisław Kostka Potocki became owners of Wilanów. Potocki, an outstanding activist of the Polish Enlightenment as well as an art connoisseur and collector, commissioned a special Neogothic gallery designed by Piotr Aigner; the gallery housed Potocki's art collection. In 1805 he made it available to the public, creating one of the first generally accessible museums in Poland. Also the surrounding of the palace was slightly changed; the park was enlarged and Romantic garden edifices designed by Aigner were placed there, (e.g. the Roman Bridge, the Chinese ar-

Wilanów, palace, southern wing,
wall facing the garden

Wilanów, palace, southern gallery,
wall facing the garden

Wilanów, palace,
tower helmet with the figure of Atlas

Wilanów, palace,
decoration of the southern alcove
viewed from the garden

bour). The two-part courtyard in front of the palace was substituted by an oval lawn.

After the death of Stanisław Kostka, the subsequent owners of the palace were his son Aleksander and grandson August. On the initiative of the latter, the second part of the northern wing of the palace was built in place of the Gothic gallery erected by his grandfather in the years 1845—1848; some changes in the interiors and around the palace were carried out: some of the edifices from this

Wilanów, palace, wall facing the garden

period are e.g.: the stone pergola by the northern wing and the bridge by the main gate, as well as the group of manèges and coach houses.

After the death of August Potocki and his wife Aleksandra, the last owners of Wilanów were the Branicki family. The palace belonged to them until 1945. In the years 1893—1906 restoration and conservation work was carried out under the supervision of Władysław Marconi, which was continued after World War I.

In 1944, with the outbreak of the Warsaw Uprising, the palace was occupied by German troops; barracks were set up in former royal chambers and the southern wings were changed over into a hospital. In the course of the withdrawing German troops, the palace was repeatedly robbed, and exceptionally precious pictures as well as carpets, silverware and ceramics were taken away.

After 1945, a permanent department of the National Museum in Warsaw was set up in Wilanów and after carrying out thorough restoration work, the palace was opened to the public in 1962. Stolen works of art were mostly recovered.

INTERIORS OF THE PALACE

The interiors of the palace comprise a group of residential chambers from the 17th, 18th and 19th centuries. The oldest, coming from the times of King Jan III, are situated in the main corpus and both galleries. Rooms for residential use were set up on the ground floor in compliance with Polish manor house tradition, not on the first floor as suggested by theoreticians of modern palace architecture. Their layout is strictly symmetrical. At the heart of the Baroque extablishment are the two storey high Great Vestibule and the Dutch Cabinet situated behind it. On both sides of the Great Vestibule and Cabinet there are former bedrooms, royal antechambers and small cabinets connected with them — Jan III's on the right, and Maria Kazimiera's on the left.

The **Great Vestibule** in Jan III's times was the main artistic and ideological place in the architecture of the palace. It was decorated with a plafond by Jerzy Eleuter Szymonowicz-Siemiginowski representing the *Allegory of*

Day and Night, where the central place is taken by the god of Day, Apollo, personifying the King himself. Opposite the main entrance to the palace is the monumental equestrian statue of Jan III as the conqueror of the Turks, which was later copied for the Łazienki Park. The Corinthian order used for dividing the walls, which similarly as on the façade symbolized respect due to the inheritor of the virtues of Roman emperors, completed this artistic apotheosis of the King. Unfortunately, the present appearance of the Great Vestibule differs much from that of Jan III's-times. The new decoration was designed by Szymon Bogumił Zug towards the end of the 18th century. The walls divided by twelve Ionic demicolumns made of goldish stucco are decorated with grey-brown stucco panels; the capitals and panel frames were made of white stucco. In the 19th century Siemiginowski's plafond was replaced by a stucco composition designed by Henryk Marconi. The statue of *Jan III*, taken away already in August II's times, now stands in the niche under the southern tower. Only the figure of the *Four Winds* in the faceted corners remained of the former

decoration.

Most features of Jan III's Baroque period were retained by both **Bedrooms** and **Antechambers**, which are decorated with plafonds representing allegories of the *Four Seasons* by Szymonowicz-Siemiginowski, made in the 1680's. A thematic completion is provided by friezes painted on canvas and placed in facets or medallions with scenes taken from Vergil's *Georgics*, which represent the tasks and pastimes of peasants, appropriate for each season and incorporated into the stuccowork. All of the decoration underlines those features of the royal country residence, which were typical of the gentry and constitutes and apotheosis of the royal pair expressed in the language of allegory. The King's bedroom is decorated with a Plafond representing *Summer*. The radiant *Phoebus* represents Jan III and the accompanying *Aurora* is Maria Kazimiera. In an allegorical way, the plafond shows their rule as full of glory and blessings for the fatherland; the framework of oak leaves surrounding the plafond symbolises royal power, while the interlocked dolphins represented in the corners are a symbol of a good and wise ruler.

113

Wilanów, palace, main corpus
— wall facing the garden

Wilanów, palace, fragment of the decoration
of the wall facing the garden

Wilanów, palace, Sybille — decoration
of the corpus of the wall facing the garden

There is a magnificent canopied bed in the King's Bedroom with attributes of a warrior — precious armour, shields and swords set with precious stones.

The Royal Antechamber preceding the bedroom is decorated with a plafond featuring a representation of *Winter*, showing the ruler of winds Aeolus subduing turbulent winds. This is a metaphor referring to Jan III, who as a powerful ruler subdues the "winds" tearing at the internal affairs of the Republic. In this Antechamber there is a portrait representing the royal family; besides Jan III and Maria Kazimiera their three sons, the Princes Jakub, Aleksander and Konstanty, as well as Jakub's wife — Jadwiga Amalia, the Duchess of Naumburg with their daughter, and the King and Queen's daughter, Princess Teresa Kunegunda. On one of the columns in the background there is a shield alluding to the Sobieskis' coat of arms — Janina.

The Queen's Bedroom and Antechamber plafonds portray respectively: *Spring*, represented as the goddes Flora scattering flowers, personifying the beauty of the Queen and the feeling of love she inspires in her subjects; *Autumn*, represented as the goddess of good harvest Pomona — she symbolises the successful influence of the Sobieskis resulting in prosperity and plentitude for the fatherland.

The walls of the royal pair's apartments are covered with Baroque tapestries of Genoese velour. They are also decorated with marble fireplaces, which have great mirrors in gilded frames. The interiors are filled with 17th century Polish, French and Dutch furniture as well as many precious works of silver, glass, and ceramic.

Of unusual interest is the decoration of the so-called **Mirror Cabinet** situated in the south-eastern alcove, which belongs to the Queen's apartments. The ceiling is decorated with a plafond by the French painter Claude Callot, representing Maria Kazimiera as *Aurora* and the King's three sons as *Winds*. The allegorical portrait of the Queen with her sons was to be an apotheosis of Maria Kazimiera as the mother of the royal family, giving birth to the inheritors of the heroic monarch. The plafond was encompassed by a magnificent stucco frame with figures of sphin-

Wilanów, garden, balustrade of the terrace and stairs

Wilanów, garden, arbour

xes, motifs of fruit bearing branches, flowers, fruits and pairs of putti carrying crowns placed in the supraportas. The decoration is in a way a completion — in the form of a Baroque allegory — of the main idea presented in the rooms, referring to the duties and obligations of the mother of the ruling family.

The **Galleries** connecting the main corpus of the palace with towers and side wings have their walls and ceiling decorated with a cycle of paintings representing the *Story of the Love between Amor and Psyche*; the paintings by Michelangelo Palloni were conceived as the allegory of Jan III's love for Maria Kazimiera, born of her spiritual and physical beauty. The Northern gallery leading to the wing housing part of Stanisław Kostka Potocki's collections is furthermore decorated with his equestrian portrait painted in 1781 by the outstanding French classicist painter Jacques Louis David. The decoration of the Baroque interiors situated on the first floor of the main corpus, was much more modest. For the most part, these were small, low cabinets, with polichrómed naked ceilings or walls decorated with paintings. Some of them are typical of the interiors of manor houses popular among the gentry in

that period. One of the more interesting rooms on the first floor is the so-called Farfurowy Cabinet, the walls of which have been lined with glazing of white cobalt imitating delftware. Amusing and interesting is also the decoration of the small *al fresco* cabinet — decorated — already during Elżbieta Sieniawska's rule in Wilanów — by the painter Józef Rossi; it includes, e.g. a small *Negro Boy Holding a Cage with a Parrot*. 18th century apartments from the times of August II and the Duchess Izabella Lubomirska are grouped mainly on the ground floor of the southern wing and in the bath pavilion which is its extension.

The most presentable and monumental interior of this part of the palace is the so-called **Great Dining-room of August II** planned around 1730 by Jan Zygmunt Deybel. It is two stories high. There are Corinthian pilasters on its walls; the double row of windows in the southern wall has its counterpart in the double row of mirrors on the opposite side. On the shorter walls, over the marble fireplaces, there are galleries for the royal orchestra. The cast iron plates in the fireplaces are decorated with the King's monograms: "A.R." (Augustus Rex) under the royal

Wilanów, palace, Great Vestibule

Wilanów, palace, the King's Bedroom

crown. The rooms are also decorated with portraits, including those of *Jan III* and *Maria Kazimiera*, as well as *August II*.

Adjacent to the Great Dining-room are apartments of the Duchess Izabella Lubomirska. Their layout — in compliance to 18th century fashion is en suite. The most interesting interior among Duchess Lubomirska's apartments is the **Bathroom** designed by Szymon Bogumił Zug. The main part of the room, the walls of which are lined with white and green marble, is the rectangular niche separated by two columns of multi-coloured stucco; in the niche a bathtub was placed on six gilded lion paws, to which water flowed from the stucco lion's muzzle situated above. The back wall of the niche had a built-in panel decorated with an illusionist fresco composition representing a Romantic landscape, which added the feeling of depth to the niche. Thanks to the placing of mirrored doors on both sides of the niche opposite the window, the effect of a visual connection of the interior with the garden was achieved. An interesting element of the Bathroom furnishings is the stucco canopy, placed on one of its si-

de walls, with bunches of white and black ostrich feathers on top. The canopy with a green material matched in colour to the interior flowing down from it, constituted the framework of the sofa-bed which was designed for rest after bathing. The bathroom was followed by two further rooms: the Bedroom and the Cabinet, all of which together comprised the so-called Bathing Apartment.

19th century apartments from the times of Stanisław Kostka Potocki are situated mainly on the ground floor of the northern wing. Next to the living chambers, there are mainly exhibition rooms of the Potockis' museum, which were restored to their original appearance.

In the **Great Crimson Room** with a ceiling supported by *Atlantes*, there is a picture gallery, and in the neighbouring Etruscan Cabinet — a collection of antique vases, while in the Lapidarium there is an exhibition of sculptures and fragments of stone Roman sarcophagi, partly coming from excavations that Stanisław Kostka, who was interested in ancient art, conducted near Naples in the 1780's.

Next to the group of residential rooms there is, on the first

Wilanów, palace, the King's Antechamber

Wilanów, palace, *Aurora*
— plafond in the Mirror Cabinet

floor of both galleries and the northern wing, the only permanent Polish portrait gallery in the country. It comprises portraits of outstanding Polish personalities from the middle of the 16th till the 19th century, including a group of 17th century coffin portraits painted on sheet metal, which were used to decorate the catafalque during funeral ceremonies — hence their shape, adjusted to the cross-section of the coffin.

Besides painted portraits, there are also sculptures portraits, madallions, miniatures painted on porcelain, as well as attributes of authority and elements of attire and armour represented in the pictures in the gallery.

GARDEN

Over subsequent centuries, the Wilanów garden, similarly to the residence itself, underwent various changes, adapting to the current fashion and taste of its owners. Its oldest part, dating back to the times of Jan III, is its central area, stretching out between the palace and the lake. It is a two level, regular Baroque garden in Italian-French style, with decorative flower beds, high double hedges and a view opening up towards the lake. The two levels of the garden are cennected by means of a double flight of stone stairs situated on the axis of the palace.

Under the stair there is a grotto. The balustrade around the upper terrace of the garden and the balustrade of the stairs is decorated with sculptured allegories of the *Four Seasons* and *Four Stages of Love* as well as representations of sphinxes and putti with baskets of flowers; the sculptures were made in the first half of the 18th century. Along the lake shore there is a several hundred metre long promenade. On the axis of the palace there is a rectangular platform decorated with four figures of Hercules towards the south of the palace and the Baroque garden there is a romantic English-Chinese park, laid out at the end of the 18th century by Duchess Izabella Lubomirska. Its central part is taken up by a large clearing with beautiful specimen of trees and bushes. In this part of the park, over a small pond dating back to the times of Jan III, there is a 19th century obelisk in memory of Stanisław Kostka and Ignacy Potocki, and — in the western part — a 17th century column with a Maltese cross on top and — on the hillock in the Western part called "Bacchus Hill" — a ceramic figure of *Victoria*. Towards the north of the palace is the two level English park set up by Stanisław Kostka Potocki at the turn of the 18th and 19th centuries. On the lake shore, on the border between the Baroque garden and the park, is the building of the pumping house supplying water for the garden fountains — this is the work of Henryk Marconi form the early 19th century. The

Wilanów, palace, northern gallery
with the portrait of Stanisław Kostka Potocki

Wilanów, palace, *al fresco* cabinet
on the first storey of the main corpus

On the following pages:

Wilanów, palace, Princess Izabella Lubomirska's Bathroom

Wilanów, palace, August II's Dining-room

Wilanów, palace, the Great Crimson Room

northern border of the park features an artificial island with a statue commemorating the battle of Raszyn fought with Austrians in 1809. The island is linked with land by an arcaded Roman Bridge erected by Piotr Aigner. Aigner was also the author of the Chinese arbour situated nearby. In the northern part of the park there is also the 18th century Orangery building with a classicist portico facing the lake and the building of the fig house behind it. In the mid 19th century a small rose garden was set up near the southern wing of the palace, separated from the Baroque garden by a cast iron pergola overgrown with grapevine and creeper roses. It is decorated with a four-leaved fountain pool with a sculptured putto and a swan. From the south, the garden is closed by a wall with decorative vases on top. Perpendicularly to the northern wing of the palace there is a rectangular garden strand divided into six parts by an octagonal fountain pool, in the middle of which there is the figure of *Triton Blowing a Horn*.

The Wilanów garden, thanks to its variety of form and the variety and high class of its decorative elements: sculptures, fountains, and small pavilions, is one of the most beautiful gardens in Poland.

CONTENTS

	Page
Introduction	3
ROYAL CASTLE	5
Interiors of the Castle	10
Castle Square	22
Sigismundus' Column	23
OLD TOWN	26
Old Town Market-place	27
City Walls	31
Mermaid Monument	32
Statue of Jan Kiliński	33
St. John's Cathedral	34
NEW TOWN	37
Church of the Visitation	37
Sacramentines' Church	38
KRAKOWSKIE PRZEDMIEŚCIE	40
St. Anne's Church	42
Figure of the Virgin Mary of Passau	46
Monument to Adam Mickiewicz	46
Carmelite Church	47
Wessels' Palace (Saxon Post Office)	48
Czartoryskis' (Potockis') Palace	48
Visitation Nuns' Church	50
Tyszkiewiczes' Palace	53
Statue of Duke Józef Poniatowski	53
University of Warsaw	54
Library Building	54
Church of the Holy Cross	57
Sztaszic' Palace	58
Monument to Nicolaus Copernicus	58
St. Alexander's Church	59
Gnińskis' Palace	60
ŁAZIENKI	63
Palace on Water	67
White House	72
Belvedere	75
Amphitheatre	75
Myślewicki Palace	77
Temple of Sybille	81
Statue of Jan Sobieski III	82
Monument to Chopin	83
CITY CENTRE	84
Warsaw Technical University	84
Aleje Jerozolimskie	86
Marching Square	88
Grand Theatre	93
Krasiński's Palace	93
Palace of Cracow Bishops	97
Primate's Palace	97
Building of Zachęta	98
Palace of the Revenues and Treasury Commission	100
WILANÓW	103
Interiors of the Palace	112
Garden	121